THE IMPORTANCE OF

Pablo Picasso

These and other titles are included in The Importance
Of biography series:

Alexander the Great
Muhammad Ali
Louis Armstrong
Clara Barton
Napoleon Bonaparte
Rachel Carson
Charlie Chaplin
Winston Churchill
Cleopatra
Christopher Columbus
Marie Curie
Amelia Earhart
Thomas Edison
Albert Einstein
Dian Fossey
Benjamin Franklin
Galileo Galilei
Martha Graham
Stephen Hawking
Jim Henson

Harry Houdini
Thomas Jefferson
Chief Joseph
Malcolm X
Margaret Mead
Michelangelo
Wolfgang Amadeus Mozart
Sir Isaac Newton
Richard M. Nixon
Georgia O'Keeffe
Louis Pasteur
Pablo Picasso
Jackie Robinson
Anwar Sadat
Margaret Sanger
John Steinbeck
Jim Thorpe
Mark Twain
H. G. Wells

THE IMPORTANCE OF

Pablo Picasso

by
Clarice Swisher

Lucent Books, P.O. Box 289011, San Diego, CA 92198-9011

Library of Congress Cataloging-in-Publication Data

Swisher, Clarice, 1933-
    The importance of Pablo Picasso / by Clarice Swisher.
        p. cm.—(The Importance of)
    Includes bibliographical references and index.
    ISBN 1-56006-062-X (alk. pap.)
    1. Picasso, Pablo, 1881–1973—Juvenile literature.   2.
Artists—France—Biography—Juvenile literature.   [1. Picasso,
Pablo, 1881–1973.   2. Artists.   3. Painting, French.   4. Paint-
ing, Modern—20th century.]   I. Title.   II. Title: Pablo Picasso.
N6853.P5S95   1995
709'.2—dc20   94-8475
[B]   CIP
                                                              AC

For Karin and Jeff

Acknowledgments

I have had the generous support of many people
during the research for and writing of this book.
In particular, I thank Lee Swisher, who read
chapters as I wrote them and engaged in
numerous conversations about Picasso and
about the manuscript. I also thank Delores
Heyer for her generous and valuable help on my
research trip to museums in Madrid, Barcelona,
southern France, and Paris.

Contents

Foreword   9

Important Dates in the Life of Pablo Picasso   10

INTRODUCTION
Revolutionizing Art   11

CHAPTER 1
Childhood, Youth, and Art Education, 1881–1898   15

CHAPTER 2
The Maturing Artist, 1898–1905   23

CHAPTER 3
Cubism: A New Art Form, 1905–1912   33

CHAPTER 4
Collages, Ballet, and a Turning Point, 1912–1922   45

CHAPTER 5
Post-Cubism Picasso, 1922–1936   53

CHAPTER 6
War and Guernica, *1936–1945*   63

CHAPTER 7
Fame and Wealth, 1945–1954   75

CHAPTER 8
A Bountiful Old Age, 1954–1973   84

CHAPTER 9
Picasso's Influence   94

Notes   99

For Further Reading   101

Additional Works Consulted   103

Index   106

Picture Credits   111

About the Author   112

Foreword

THE IMPORTANCE OF biography series deals with individuals who have made a unique contribution to history. The editors of the series have deliberately chosen to cast a wide net and include people from all fields of endeavor. Individuals from politics, music, art, literature, philosophy, science, sports, and religion are all represented. In addition, the editors did not restrict the series to individuals whose accomplishments have helped change the course of history. Of necessity, this criterion would have eliminated many whose contribution was great, though limited. Charles Darwin, for example, was responsible for radically altering the scientific view of the natural history of the world. His achievements continue to impact the study of science today. Others, such as Chief Joseph of the Nez Percé, played a pivotal role in the history of their own people. While Joseph's influence does not extend much beyond the Nez Percé, his nonviolent resistance to white expansion and his continuing role in protecting his tribe and his homeland remain an inspiration to all.

These biographies are more than factual chronicles. Each volume attempts to emphasize an individual's contributions both in his or her own time and for posterity. For example, the voyages of Christopher Columbus opened the way to European colonization of the New World. Unquestionably, his encounter with the New World brought monumental changes to both Europe and the Americas in his day. Today, however, the broader impact of Columbus's voyages is being critically scrutinized. *Christopher Columbus,* as well as every biography in The Importance Of series, includes and evaluates the most recent scholarship available on each subject.

Each author includes a wide variety of primary and secondary source quotations to document and substantiate his or her work. All quotes are footnoted to show readers exactly how and where biographers derive their information, as well as provide stepping stones to further research. These quotations enliven the text by giving readers eyewitness views of the life and times of each individual covered in The Importance Of series.

Finally, each volume is enhanced by photographs, bibliographies, chronologies, and comprehensive indexes. For both the casual reader and the student engaged in research, The Importance Of biographies will be a fascinating adventure into the lives of people who have helped shape humanity's past, present, and will continue to shape its future.

Important Dates in the Life of Pablo Picasso

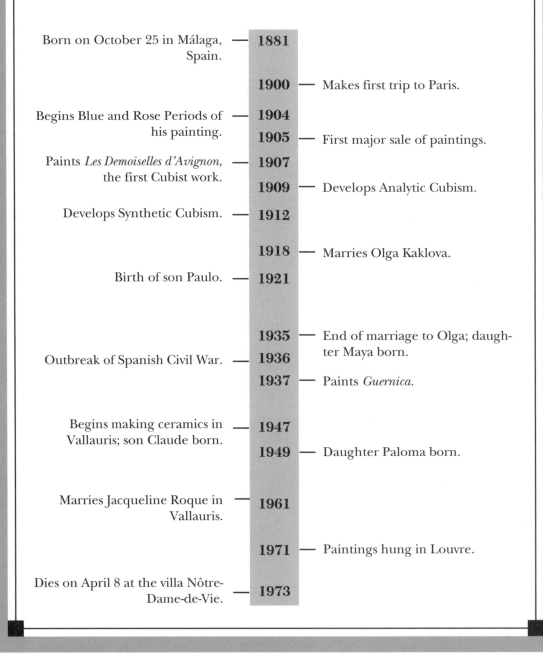

Born on October 25 in Málaga, Spain. — **1881**

1900 — Makes first trip to Paris.

Begins Blue and Rose Periods of his painting. — **1904**

1905 — First major sale of paintings.

Paints *Les Demoiselles d'Avignon*, the first Cubist work. — **1907**

1909 — Develops Analytic Cubism.

Develops Synthetic Cubism. — **1912**

1918 — Marries Olga Kaklova.

Birth of son Paulo. — **1921**

1935 — End of marriage to Olga; daughter Maya born.

Outbreak of Spanish Civil War. — **1936**

1937 — Paints *Guernica*.

Begins making ceramics in Vallauris; son Claude born. — **1947**

1949 — Daughter Paloma born.

Marries Jacqueline Roque in Vallauris. — **1961**

1971 — Paintings hung in Louvre.

Dies on April 8 at the villa Nôtre-Dame-de-Vie. — **1973**

Revolutionizing Art

When Pablo Picasso showed the first Cubist painting, *Les Demoiselles d'Avignon (The Young Ladies of Avignon)*, to his friends, even they thought it was no better than rubbish. A few years later when his Cubist works were first exhibited in London, one reviewer said they looked like children's scrawls, filled with harsh colors and lacking artistic form. A *Times* (London) reviewer thought the paintings looked like diagrams for a scientific idea that he did not understand. Sixty years later, however, another *Times* (London) reviewer called Picasso the most influential artist of his age, a genius of draftsmanship.

Twentieth-century artist Pablo Picasso revolutionized painting and changed the direction of modern art. When he was twenty-five years old, he created a new form of painting, characterized by geometric shapes and distorted figures. Artists observed that Picasso had painted in "little cubes," and the new form of painting became known as Cubism.

Pablo Picasso, creator of Cubism, is shown here with a painting characteristic of Cubist art. This painting is composed of geometric shapes that distort the subject.

Picasso's paintings did not reflect reality. He believed that through abstraction artists could capture an alternate, more powerful reality on canvas. With paintings like Café at Royan, *Picasso engrosses the viewer in color and form while expanding the definition of art.*

Before Picasso, most artists tried to re-create reality in their work, what is seen in a photograph, out the window, or in a mirror. But Picasso and a few others thought that the artist could do something greater—paint a new kind of reality. "Art," he said, "is a lie that makes us realize truth."

Art is a lie in that the artist does not imitate reality exactly. The distortion, however, can make the viewer see the truth of suffering, happiness, love, and memory, often more powerfully than can the sim-ple realism of a photograph. On the flat surface of a canvas, the artist's distortion can also make the viewer aware of move-ment, color, size, weight, and distance. Picasso's transformations of reality shocked viewers who thought his works destroyed what was familiar; in spite of their shock, however, they recognized his talent.

Picasso began drawing as a young child and painted until his death at age ninety-one. During his lifetime he pro-duced some fifteen thousand works of art, using a wide variety of media and techniques. He used oil and watercolor, sometimes combining the pigments with sand or sawdust. He drew in ink, pencil, and crayon. He made many kinds of etchings. He created sculptures in plaster, wood, bronze, and cement. He made constructions of wrought iron, wood, paper, and sheet metal. He made ceramic objects. And he designed theatrical costumes, curtains, and sets. People asked him how he could do so much and master so many techniques. He answered, according to author Dore Ashton, "Where do I get this power of creating and forming? I don't know. I have only one thought: work. I paint just as I breathe. When I work, I relax; not doing anything or entertaining

At work at a kiln, Picasso adds the finishing touches to his ceramics.

visitors makes me tired. It's often 3:00 A.M. when I switch off my light."[1]

Picasso's artistic career did not progress in neatly defined stages. He often worked on several kinds of art at a time. During the years before Cubism, for example, he painted portraits and impressions of city scenes, used only the color blue for a time, and then painted in pink. After he had developed Cubism, his style varied even more: he made realistic line drawings and portraits; he experimented with Cubist forms; he created collages; he made variations on classical works of ancient Greece and Rome; he applied Cubist ideas to sculpture. Sometimes he abandoned a subject for several years and returned to it with a new variation. Guitars, bulls, an artist in a studio, children and mothers, views from windows, and swimmers appear, disappear, and reappear in his works. Picasso refused to be bound by any particular form, choosing the one best suited to his subject.

Creative Energy

Picasso's creative genius was evident from the beginning. His first recorded words were "piz, piz," for *lapiz*, the Spanish word for pencil. As a preschooler he drew designs with a stick in the sandy walks of his play area. Picasso's father, José Ruiz, an art teacher, taught his son to draw. José Ruiz liked birds and kept cages of pigeons. He had his son draw birds and human hands until he was satisfied that the boy could draw accurately.

Throughout his life abundance and creative energy characterized the way Picasso lived. He lived in many places in

Spain and France. His studios became filled with paintings, objects to paint, books and papers, and dust. When his studios were too full, Picasso moved to new ones, usually larger. He collected many friends: art dealers, artists, collectors, poets, friends from his past, and, always, women. His personality was intense, well represented by his dark, piercing eyes. His anger was fierce; his giving, generous; his will, iron. He feared aging and hated death. When trouble occurred, he immersed himself in his work. "Painting is stronger than I am. It makes me do what it wishes," he wrote in one of his sketchbooks.

Picasso's creative genius lasted his lifetime. A friend who visited the seventy-five-year-old Picasso described him as full of life and humor. He told her he was just beginning.

In the twentieth century Picasso stands apart as the one artist most responsible for redirecting the course of art, as Michelangelo had done in his time. After Picasso had developed Cubism, many artists used the style and went on to modify it. As a pioneer of new artistic forms, Picasso was often alone. In 1976, only three years after Picasso's death, biographer Patrick O'Brian called Picasso "a historic monument, [one who] carried on with his lonely, prolific [fruitful] investigation of reality, or as he often said, of truth, still in a state of permanent, personal revolution. He was a presence of much greater value than any school [of art]."[2]

1 Childhood, Youth, and Art Education, 1881–1898

Pablo Picasso was born in Málaga, a city in southern Spain, on October 25, 1881, the first child of María Picasso y Lopez and José Ruíz Blasco. Though Pablo Picasso later remembered few events from his ten years in Málaga, this Mediterranean coastal city nonetheless made a lasting im-

Pablo Picasso, pictured here with his sister Lola in 1888, shared his family's love of art. Encouraged in his artistic endeavors, Picasso displayed his keen abilities at a young age.

pression on him. When Picasso was a child, Málaga, with its warm and sunny climate, had 120,000 people, a bullring seating 10,000, and the sounds of Gypsy flamenco music in the air. All his life Picasso loved the Mediterranean world of sun, sea, and bustling activity.

Picasso grew up in a middle-class, artistic family. Picasso's grandfather Diego Ruiz wanted to be a painter and a musician, but he worked as a glove maker to support his family. Two uncles and an aunt were amateur artists. Picasso's father was a professor at Málaga's art school, Escuela de Artes y Oficios de San Telmo, and curator of the Málaga art museum. There he restored works of art and used a studio, where he decorated fans and painted pictures of birds and flowers, which he sold or traded for rent. Though his painting lacked inspiration, he was a master craftsman.

The Boy Artist

In Málaga the Picasso family lived in a flat, or apartment, fifty stairs up from the street. Here Picasso learned to walk by pushing a large, filled, tin biscuit container. He said later that the biscuit tin

Picasso's father, Don José Ruiz Blasco, greatly influenced his artistic talents. A master craftsman and teacher, Don José was Picasso's first art teacher, training him to draw in a realistic style.

symbolized his ability to grasp people's inner feelings. Picasso had two younger sisters, Concepción and Lolita, called Lola. Outside their flat, gardens, benches, and sandy walks provided a playground for the three children. With a stick Picasso made floral and geometric designs in the sand. He drew, tracing the entire shape with one line, ending at the starting point. All his life he had the unusual skill of being able to start a drawing at any point, as he had practiced as a child.

Picasso played an art game with his sisters and cousins. They chose an animal and named the place for Picasso to start. With either scissors or a pencil, Picasso could quickly produce the chosen animal. He did not draw stick figures as other chil-

dren do; his earliest scrawls showed an ability to see in the sophisticated way adults see. His family admired and supported his desire to draw. Admiring girl cousins, an adoring mother, and many doting aunts surrounded Picasso. Don José also doted on his son. He took young Pablo to bullfights and allowed him to help clean his brushes. From all this special attention, Picasso developed into a stubborn, self-willed child, to whom authority meant nothing.

At school, teachers and students also viewed Picasso as exceptional and thought he functioned on a plane different from other children. If he got up to look out the window, teachers did not correct him. Usually he sat drawing pigeons and bulls and waiting to be released from his school prison. He learned little about reading, writing, or arithmetic there. He struggled to learn to count and to tell time, and he treated numbers as if they were shapes to be drawn. He did not do the dull, repetitive exercises in grammar, spelling, and handwriting. But his father seemed unworried about his son's poor school performance.

Don José was Picasso's first art teacher, training him to draw with photographic realism. He gave Pablo a solid, disciplined basis in drawing by pinning real pigeon feet on a board and requiring the boy to draw them until he reproduced them accurately. Picasso became a receptive art pupil who respected his artist father. Biographer Patrick O'Brian quotes Picasso, speaking many years later: "Every time I draw a man, automatically I think of my father. . . . As far as I am concerned *the man* is Don José, and that will be so as long as I live. . . . He had a beard. . . . I see all men I draw with his features, more or less."[3]

Because Picasso liked to save things, some of his Málaga drawings and paintings still exist. The earliest, from 1890 or 1891, is a little painting of a picador, the horseman in a bullfight who cuts the bull's neck muscle so that the bull will keep its head low. Picasso painted the picador in oil on the cover taken off a cigar box, since his father did not yet allow him to use canvases. Biographer Patrick O'Brian describes the painting:

> It shows a burly man in yellow seated upon a little miserable bony blindfolded old horse up against the pink barrier of the bull-ring. The spectators, two men . . . and an opulent [wealthy] woman, are so large that they make the horse look even more wretchedly small. The horse is unpadded—the eight-or-nine-year-old Pablo had already seen some dozens disemboweled in the arena—and the picador with his armored leg sits right down in the deep Spanish saddle. The two are remarkably well observed; and my impression is that they are observed quite objectively: but I may be mistaken; there may be compassion for the horse.[4]

All of the eyes in this little painting are holes, which Lola made while playing with a nail, giving the figures fixed stares.

Life in La Coruña

About the time Picasso painted the picador, the museum in Málaga closed. Don José found a job as an art teacher at Instituto da Guarda, a secondary school in La Coruña, a town on the Atlantic coast of northwestern Spain. He moved his family at the end of the summer of 1891, arriving in La Coruña at the beginning of the autumn storms. A small export town, La Coruña is exposed to great winds that sweep in from the Atlantic Ocean. From fall to spring, the weather is a mixture of fog, rain, and wind, unlike the sunny weather in Málaga. La Coruña lies within Galicia, a state near Portugal that has a language much like Portuguese. Picasso could not understand it and experienced for the first time the feeling of being an outsider.

In La Coruña Picasso attended the art school where his father taught. Don José taught Picasso the techniques of pen-and-ink drawing, charcoal, crayon, oil, and

Picasso's portrait of his father, The Artist's Father, *is a respectful rendition.*

watercolor. He was a strict teacher, demanding discipline and hard work. From his father's instruction Picasso developed the natural powers of his hands and eyes and increased his ability to observe. By this time, also, Picasso had stopped being the spoiled brat of the Málaga house and readily accepted his father's instruction. Soon young Picasso won recognition as the school's outstanding artist.

Picasso spent the dark, dismal days in La Coruña drawing and painting. He drew the city tower, the local people, animals, and pigeons. He made cartoons of skirts blowing in the wind. Instead of writing to his relatives in Málaga, he drew a news sheet every Sunday and added jokes about the weather. Separated from the Mediterranean sun and his relatives, Picasso developed a special interest in animals. Unlike children who have such stuffed toys as floppy-eared bunnies, Picasso saw wild gutter cats, bulls gored in the bullring, and other animals living according to cruel human codes that contained no notion of comfort. He later

painted people whose lives were just as cruel and comfortless.

It was in La Coruña that both Picasso and his father realized that the son was the better artist. Discouraged by his life in La Coruña, Don José often began sketches and then turned them over to Picasso. One evening when Don José was on a walk, Picasso finished his father's sketch of a pigeon. He completed the claws and the leg feathers with such skill that Don José knew he could never do as well. He turned his palette and his brushes over to his thirteen-year-old son and vowed that he would never paint again. Though the incident increased young Picasso's confidence, he was still too immature to understand his father's mixed feelings. Don José was proud of his son's talent but humiliated that the youth was better at the work he had chosen and loved. This awkward change in roles confused Picasso and led him to say cruel things, even though he loved his father.

During this time in La Coruña, Picasso's sister Concepción became seriously ill with diphtheria. Picasso bargained with

God: If God let his sister live, he would give up his artistic gift and never paint again. After some thought, however, he realized that he was torn between wanting to save his sister and wanting to save his art. When Concepción died, Picasso concluded that God must be evil. How, he wondered, could God have let his sister die when he had offered to give up his art. Arianna Huffington explains:

> His guilt was enormous. . . . And it was compounded by his almost magical conviction that his little sister's death had released him to be a painter and follow the call of the powers he had been given, whatever the consequences.[5]

This experience was only the first of many battles that went on within Picasso's conscience, times that brought doubt, disappointment, and despair.

Life in Barcelona

During the summer of 1895, Don José exchanged jobs with a Barcelona art teacher who wanted to return to La Coruña. Picasso's family returned to the Mediterranean sun. Picasso packed his pictures of La Coruña, his sketchbooks, and his portraits, some of which he had shown in his first one-person exhibition in the doorway of an umbrella maker's shop. Though the four years in La Coruña had held unhappy experiences for the family, Picasso's art had developed, with a firm foundation in techniques.

Among his favorite pictures were *Girl with Bare Feet* and studies of La Coruña beggars. Curator Hélène Seckel describes

Picasso completed Girl with Bare Feet, *one of his favorite paintings, at the age of thirteen.*

the painting of a girl only slightly younger than Picasso:

> He painted this sad-faced, weary, and slightly sullen street-urchin. Certain features of this portrait are striking for their unconventionality; deliberately stressed, certain details take on a particular importance: the bare feet ("the children of the poor in our country always went about barefoot, and this little girl's feet were covered with sores," Picasso later recalled), the large, ungainly hands, the unsymmetric features of the face, with one cheek puffier than the other, and the slightly cross-eyed gaze of the very dissimilar eyes.[6]

The portrait of a beggar, *Man in a Cap*, portrays another sad-faced person. The thin face and pathetic eyes complement the need expressed by the outstretched hand. The folds and shadows of the beggar's clothing are particularly realistic.

Don José moved his family south to Barcelona in the state of Catalonia, where he became a professor at La Lonja, the Barcelona School of Fine Arts. An old seaport, Barcelona in 1895 had a population of a half million people and had become a cultural center. Its people had a reputation for working hard to be successful in a resource-poor area. They had a proverb, according to author Patrick O'Brian: "From a stone the Catalan will draw

Man in a Cap is characteristic of Picasso's earlier, more realistic paintings.

bread."[7] In this new city where the fashions and the language were unlike those in either Málaga or La Coruña, Picasso again felt like an outsider.

At La Lonja, the fourteen-year-old Picasso applied for entrance into the higher classes designed for students twenty years old or older. He took the academy's rigorous tests—creating two drawings, one of a school model draped in a sheet and another of a standing nude. Though the school gave students a month to complete the drawings, Picasso finished them in one day and received entrance to the advanced classes in the academy. Biographer Pierre Daix reports that of one of the drawings, Picasso said, "I finished mine the first day. . . . I studied it for a long time, and I carefully considered what I could still add to it, but I couldn't see a thing. Absolutely nothing."[8] In this school he was again considered extraordinary, a person to whom the regular rules did not apply. He became close friends with art student Manuel Pallarès, who continued to be his friend for many years.

Picasso drew not only in his rigorous art courses, but during his free time. He was determined to improve his skill at capturing the atmosphere of a street scene or a person's feelings. He filled sketchbooks with bullfights, animals, streetwalkers, beggars, and soldiers. He drew and painted his mother, his father, his sister Lola, and himself. Among his many pictures were a dozen or more with religious themes. During this period his paintings developed a similarity to the works of French Impressionist painters, who emphasized the effect of light on a subject.

Early in 1897 Picasso, then fifteen, painted his first important Impressionist-style work, *Science and Charity*. A large oil

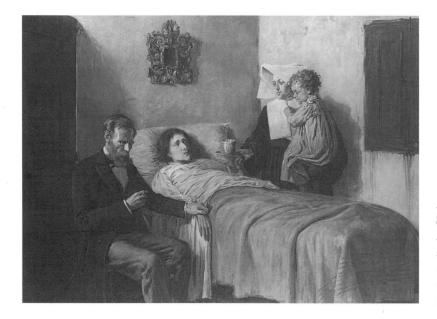

Painted at age fifteen, Science and Charity *was Picasso's first significant Impressionist-style work. This complex painting explores the mixed emotions of a sick woman's caregivers.*

painting measuring 8 by 6½ feet, the painting shows a sick woman in bed. On one side of the bed a nun holds a child and offers a cup of soup; on the other side a doctor takes the patient's pulse. The painting represents two kinds of care given to a sick woman. The doctor brings scientific knowledge, and the nun brings nourishment and tenderness. Done in grays, black, white, and subdued warm colors, the painting shows light illuminating the room from the upper left and highlighting the faces, the mirror, and the bed covering. Each face conveys a particular emotion. Before settling on the composition for *Science and Charity*, Picasso painted a watercolor sketch and three oil studies.

Influence of Els Quatre Gats and Horta de Ebro

After Picasso had become acquainted in Barcelona, he spent his time at a café called Els Quatre Gats (The Four Cats). Here, painters, intellectuals, and writers gathered to discuss Spanish politics, French Impressionist art, German philosophy, and *modernismo*, the modern way of art. The café sponsored concerts and exhibited local artists' works. Picasso had a one-man show at Els Quatre Gats, but neither the public nor the critics paid attention. He received more attention for the poster and the menu cover he designed for the café. By age eighteen Picasso was accepted as the leading figure of those who gathered there because he was the best artist, even though he was penniless and still unknown outside his close circle of friends. His teenage years in Barcelona and the friends he made there shaped his personality and his art. Years later he gave nearly all of his early pictures to the museum in Barcelona because he still felt attached to the city.

Picasso's art-school friend, Pallarès, invited Picasso to visit him in Horta de Ebro, a farming village far inland in the mountains. They had to travel the last miles on foot, using a mule to haul the painting supplies. Pallarès's family had farmed the land there since ancient times. Later Picasso often said that everything he knew he learned in Pallarès's village. He learned to use a scythe to cut grain; how to make wine and oil; how to harvest hay; and how to shear sheep, butcher pigs, and milk cows. The village folk liked Picasso and included him in their work, but he was an awkward city boy, and they had to take the pitchfork away from him. In the fall and winter Picasso shared the townspeople's feasts on All Hallows Day, Christmas, and Saint Anthony's Day, the day animals were brought to the church to be blessed. In Horta, Picasso acquired new values, a broader understanding of the world, and fluency in the Catalan language. His drawing became stronger, with more attention to texture and to light and dark shading, as shown in several fine drawings of sheep and goats.

After eight months in Horta de Ebro, Picasso returned to Barcelona, where he again joined the conversations at Els Quatre Gats and further developed his ideas about politics, philosophy, and art. However, he had begun to think of Paris. He believed that art was on the other side of the Pyrenees, the mountains that lie between Spain and France, and Barcelona no longer inspired him.

2 The Maturing Artist, 1898–1905

After returning from Horta, Picasso lived with a succession of friends in meager studios and rooms, since he had no income or family allowance. By 1899 his painting technique was mature, but the teenage Picasso still lacked personal and intellectual maturity. He was desperately unhappy at times, and moody. And he was undecided about a signature for his paintings. At first he signed his paintings P. Ruiz; for a time after 1895 he signed them P. Ruiz Picasso. Finally, he chose Picasso, his mother's name, and dropped Ruiz. His friends, who thought Picasso was less common, encouraged his decision.

The gatherings at Els Quatre Gats became increasingly important to Picasso's developing ideas. The intellectuals and artists who gathered there reappeared throughout Picasso's life; among them were Isidro Nonell, Carlos Casagemas, Carlos Junyer, Manolo, Jaime Sabartés, Santiago Rusiñol, and Miguel Utrillo. Among other things, these men discussed the social conditions of Barcelona's poor, and they opposed the authoritative system that caused misery and injustice for the helpless. Because Picasso had not been a good student and had read little, he listened as his friends discussed writers such as Tolstoy and Ibsen and philosophers such as Nietzsche.

In Portrait de Sabartés, *Picasso extends the boundaries of art with his use of Modernism. He believed that through this modern art movement he could enlarge the idea of beauty.*

Picasso was especially interested in discussions about art and *modernismo*, the emerging way of art. He came to believe that it was his destiny to push out the boundaries of art and to enlarge the idea of beauty. Biographer O'Brian reports that he said, "To me [*beauty*] is a word without sense because I do not know where its meaning comes from nor where it leads to."[9] It took him ten years to work out the ideas that began simmering in 1899 in Barcelona. During this time he looked to both art of the past and contemporary art to help clarify his views. He incorporated into his work aspects of many different periods of art. But as biographer Pierre Daix says, "Whenever we track down some influence, we find that he mastered it and went beyond."[10]

Picasso's First Trip to Paris

Early in 1900 Picasso became increasingly impatient with Barcelona life. His interest lay in Paris, where some of his friends had already gone. In the fall of 1900, just before his nineteenth birthday, Picasso and Casagemas, his friend from the Gats, took a train to Paris. The two young men met Isidro Nonell, a Gats friend, who offered them his studio and helped Picasso sell three paintings he had brought from Barcelona.

Then Picasso set about to discover Paris. He had arrived just in time for the World's Fair art show, a retrospective of modern art. A retrospective is an exhibition that includes artists' works from the beginning of their painting careers. Picasso saw the works of the nineteenth-century masters van Gogh, Gauguin, Cézanne, Toulouse-Lautrec, and Degas. In addition, he went to small galleries and to the Louvre, Paris's major art museum, where he studied the old masters of painting. With other Spanish painters and sculptors, all just as poor, he explored

Paris cafés and dance halls and cabarets, or nightclubs. In nighttime Paris he found wonderful subjects for painting. By a stroke of fortune he met a wealthy Catalan industrialist named Pere Manyac, who offered to pay Picasso a hundred and fifty francs a month for all the artwork he could produce. That salary certainly did not make him rich—the poor in Paris had about ninety francs a month, the comfortable above four hundred—but Picasso was relieved to have a steady income.

During this first trip to Paris Picasso tried to absorb as much from the city and its artists as he could. Because he had not found his own style, he tried out styles of other painters. He liked the works of Renoir, who had painted *Le Moulin de la Galette* in 1876, and Toulouse-Lautrec, who had painted *At the Moulin Rouge* in 1892. Picasso's first Paris painting was *Le Moulin de la Galette*. Like the earlier two artists, Picasso painted a café full of people dancing

Paintings by Toulouse-Lautrec inspired Picasso and helped him to find his own artistic style. Toulouse-Lautrec's La Goule *is shown here.*

While in Paris, Picasso painted his own version (pictured) of Renoir's Le Moulin de la Galette. *Like Renoir, Picasso used the contrast of light and dark to emphasize the mood of his work.*

and sitting at tables. Like them, he contrasted dark colors with brightly illuminated faces, tabletops, and glasses. He also painted street scenes and impressions of unusual individuals and couples enjoying each other's company.

Picasso's first Paris trip ended when he and Casagemas went to Barcelona for the holidays. After the new year, Picasso painted in Madrid for two months, but his friend Casagemas returned to Paris. There he shot himself dead on February 17, 1901, because of despair over a failed romance with a woman. The event caused great suffering for Picasso, who found expression for his grief by painting his friend in a burial scene and by using him as a figure in many other works.

More Trips to Paris

Between 1901 and 1904 Picasso made two more trips to Paris. During this period he was extremely poor and lived in squalid conditions, sharing small rooms with others. On both trips Picasso often went hungry. There are stories of his eating putrid sausages and peddling paintings to buy food. More than once Picasso burned drawings to keep warm in his cold Paris room. Sometimes he had neither canvases nor paint and had to make do with poor-quality materials or stop painting altogether.

While struggling to find his own way in art, Picasso lived an active social life, but he painted alone. He went out all night to Paris music halls and cafés and developed a reputation as a cheerful and charming friend. But he felt none of the carefree spirit he may have appeared to have. He was still haunted by the tortured life and suicide of Casagemas. Moreover, his mind was full of doubt and inner conflict about his work. When a painter needs intense concentration, he must work in solitude, and since Picasso wanted to find a new way in art, he was particularly alone.

To avoid the risk of letting artists of the time influence him, he went to places where he could study life firsthand. He wanted to find what lay behind the human faces other artists were painting. Out on the streets he saw beggars, poor women and children, blind men, lunatics, and outcasts. Years later Picasso remembered this period as the hardest time he ever experienced; he felt his own hunger and cold, and even more, he felt disgust at the poverty he saw around him. He felt deeply discouraged about his destiny as an artist. But "the man whose iron determination to express himself as he saw fit could not be broken by any force whatsoever, certainly not poverty, discouragement, . . . or persuasion. [He had an] incorruptible strength of purpose," says biographer Patrick O'Brian.[11] His friend from Gats, Jaime Sabertés, explained Picasso's philosophy at the time: that art was the child of sadness and pain, that unhappiness suited reflection and contemplation, and that pain was the basis of life.

Toward the end of 1901 Picasso began to rely on the color blue to express his thoughts and experiences. He had noticed the blues Toulouse-Lautrec had used to create indoor scenes with artificial lighting, and he tried a painting like them. *The Blue Room* (1901) shows a woman standing in her room, washing. Artificial light illuminates her bare skin, her bed, and a wall,

Picasso Arrives in Paris

At nineteen Picasso, with his friend Casagemas, arrived in Paris with little money, an armful of paintings, and no place to live. In Picasso: Pablo Ruiz Picasso: A Biography, *Patrick O'Brian describes what the young Spaniards found.*

"It was Paris. A Paris as dirty as Barcelona or even dirtier but infinitely more full of color: brilliant posters everywhere . . . : sandwichmen; women dressed in bright colors rather than the black of Spain; startling umbrellas. Everywhere the enormous roar of the iron tires of horse-busses, drays, carts, and wagons on the crowded stone-paved streets, littered deep with dung, speckled with the bills handed out by the sandwichmen and thrown away; and mingling with the accustomed omnipresent [all-pervasive] reek of horse-piss and dung, the sharp smell of petrol fumes. . . . A bewildering great city vaster by far than Barcelona or Madrid, and immensely active—no leisurely Spanish pacing here: the French language all round them, a babel of signs, street-cries, directions, people talking, policemen, carters, cab-drivers bawling in their native tongue; and Picasso, the eternal outsider, did not possess a word of it."

In paintings such as The Blue Room, *Picasso portrays the modest life of the poor, while also experimenting with lines, shapes, and colors. This period is known as Picasso's Blue Period.*

on which a Toulouse-Lautrec poster hangs. Although the painting is done primarily in blue, Picasso also used reds and yellows in the flowers and the fabrics on the bed and in the rug. Picasso had yet to rely entirely on blue.

The Blue Period

But soon, during what art historians call his Blue Period, Picasso relied almost entirely on the color blue. He realized the power that blue gave—blue shadows, blue hair, blue catching a special light on naked flesh. In some of his blue paintings, a cold blue drowns out all other colors, and in others blue creates a tender, warm tone. The blue paintings done in Barcelona in 1902 concentrate on single, downtrodden characters living in intolera-

ble conditions. With these paintings he tried to accomplish two goals. First, he wanted to paint unglamorous life and poor people in an objective way, showing them just as they were. Second, he wanted to experiment with lines, shapes, and the many effects of blue.

He painted the portrait *Célestine* (1903) almost in monochrome, or one color—a midnight blue for the woman's cloak, a lighter shade for the plain background, and the same shades and some yet lighter to make the shadows of her face and the spot of her marred eye. Only a hint of pink shows on her left cheek. In *The Old Guitarist* (1903) a frail old man in tattered clothes sits cross-legged on a street trying to strum his guitar. In *The Woman Ironing* (1904) a weary-looking woman stands, ironing a garment on a board. In these last two paintings Picasso experimented with line to create rectangular

In The Old Guitarist, *painted in 1908, Picasso accentuates the features of a downtrodden man through the use of varying shades of blue.*

spaces for the figures. In both he used shades of blue. Both figures have elongated hands and necks; both have cramped postures; both portray the starkness of broken human bodies. Neither painting tells a whole story; both depict the blue of misery, a blue without hope. Art critic Miguel Utrillo says that in the blue paintings, Picasso "does not pardon the weaknesses of people of our time, and brings out even the beauties of the horrible."[12]

In the spring of 1904 Picasso settled in Paris on Butte Montmartre in one of the tenement, or apartment, houses nick-named Bateau-Lavoir ("the floating laun-

dry"). He furnished his little studio, a painter's cabin, with a legless sofa, a table, a rusty iron stove, a trunk, and an oil lamp. Picasso was still poor and life was hard, forcing him on occasion to sell a painting to junk dealer Père Soulié for cash. He dressed in plumber's clothes because they were durable. In spite of his poverty he had a pet mouse, three cats, a dog, and a little monkey. At one time the owner of the art supply store cut off his credit, and he had to paint over canvases already painted. One watercolor, *The Madman* (1904) done in mannerist style (a style distorting scale and perspective) shows where Picasso pasted two pieces of paper together when he had no long sheets. Again he burned sketches to keep warm.

Bateau-Lavoir

Bateau-Lavoir was like Els Quatre Gats, a center for intellectuals and artists. Among Picasso's friends were prominent art critics, writers, actors, and artists. There was one mathematician who explained Albert Einstein's theory of relativity and the fourth dimension when it was published in 1905. This group discussed, socialized, and ate together, often meeting at the Café Agile. Picasso liked to organize trips for them to go to the nearby circus, the Médrano. Attracted by the smell of the animals and the professionalism of the performers, Picasso attended three or four times a week. The performances reminded him of scenes from Spanish fairs.

In a rainstorm in August 1904, Picasso met Fernande Olivier, who became his companion for six years and a model for his art. Four months older than Picasso,

Pablo Picasso and Fernande Olivier (below), who was Picasso's companion for six years. Picasso's apartment house and studio, Bateau-Lavoir (left), attracted intellectuals and artists.

she was beautiful, intelligent, and lazy. Biographer Patrick O'Brian says: "Picasso's pictures show a large, placid woman, with a beautiful complexion and great almond eyes . . . sensual: natural and at ease."[13] She came into Picasso's hard life when he was destitute, and she brought a new inspiration that soon appeared as the pink colors in his paintings. Biographer Alfred H. Barr Jr. quotes Fernande Olivier's impression of Picasso when she first met him. She saw Picasso as

> small, dark, thickset, unquiet, disquieting, with somber eyes, deepset, piercing, strange, almost motionless. Awkward gestures, the hands of a woman, badly dressed, careless. A thick lock of hair, black and glossy cut across his intelligent obstinate forehead. Half bo-hemian [unconventional], half work-man in his clothes, his long hair brushing the collar of his tired coat.[14]

Throughout 1904 Picasso changed the subject matter, the color, and the tone of his painting. Before 1904 blues had por-

trayed anguish, and he had painted morbid subjects. After 1904 he painted wanderers and exiles in pinks and earth tones. The figures are circus entertainers, acrobats, and poor and alienated families. Unlike the victims of the Blue Period, they display strength and pride. The figures of the Pink, or Rose, Period are lean and muscular, with agile and graceful movements. Picasso composed them in curved and oval spaces.

In A Picasso Anthology: Documents, Criticism, Reminiscences, *Marilyn McCully quotes Fernande Olivier's description of her introduction to Picasso and his work.*

"As I lived in the same house as he did I often bumped into him. At this period he seemed to spend all his time on the little Montmartre square, and I remember thinking: 'Whenever does he work?' I learned later that he preferred painting at night, so as not to be disturbed. During the day he was visited by a constant stream of Spaniards. I met Picasso as I was coming home one thundery evening. He was holding a tiny kitten in his arms, and he held it out to me, laughing and blocking my path. I laughed, too, and he took me to see his studio.

This was the introduction into the world in which I was to live for so long; the world I came to know, love and respect."

The Pink Period

The same figures appeared in several paintings in Picasso's Pink Period. In *Two Acrobats with a Dog* (1905) two young boys stand with their dog in a barren landscape. Wearing their performing costumes, the young wanderers stare into space without expression and seem headed nowhere. Their faces reveal none of the suffering depicted in the blue pictures. The background contains warm tans and grays, and their costumes contain shades of pink. A line enclosing the space taken up by the two boys and the dog makes an oval, unlike the rectangular space enclosing the guitarist and the woman ironing.

The two acrobats appear again in the most fascinating painting of the Pink Period. A large canvas—84 by 90 inches—*The Family of Saltimbanques* (1905) shows a wandering circus stopped in the same barren landscape. The painting suggests no reason for their stopping and gives no indication of time. Are they traveling to a new place? Have they just performed? These details matter less than the painting's artistic qualities. The composition is built on a spiral that unwinds from left to right. The spiral begins with a small girl seen from behind, whose pink dress and shoes identify her as a dancer. The spiral moves left to a tall Harlequin, painted with Picasso's features and wearing a black, tan, red, and gray costume. The curve then moves around to a stout man, a *saltimbanque* (a tumbler) in a red costume and hat, speaking as if he were in command. Two boys, the acrobats, with shaded eyes, stand by waiting. The curve ends with a seated girl in a hat, seated there with no apparent purpose and with no apparent connection to the group. She is connected to the stout man, however, in that both wear hats and both hold their left arms in similar positions. The figures display little emotion or connection to one another.

The Family of Saltimbanques inspired German poet Rainer Maria Rilke, who knew Picasso, to write about the figures in the fifth section of his *Duino Elegies:*

> But tell me, who *are* they, these acrobats, even a little
> more fleeting than we ourselves,—
> so urgently, ever since childhood,
> wrung by an (oh, for the sake of whom?)
> never-contented will? That keeps

on wringing them,
bending them, slinging them,
swinging them,
throwing them and catching them back.[15]

Ancient Greek Models

In 1905, on a trip to Holland, Picasso became interested in the problem of representing weight and substance. His circus figures were thin and agile; now he saw Dutch women who looked plump. Painted in blues and pinks, the figures in *Three Dutch Women* (1905) have full arms and hips and stand with feet planted firmly on the ground. After that trip Picasso continued to pursue his interest in weight and

The unusual composition of The Family of Saltim-banques, *painted during Picasso's Pink Period, makes it one of Picasso's most intriguing works.*

In Three Dutch Women *Picasso experimented with representing weight and substance.*

substance by turning to the classical art of the ancient Greeks. Incorporating qualities from the Greek tradition, he painted figures in studied poses, more solid in shape, and with simpler colors. *La Toilette* (1905 or 1906) shows Picasso's most complete mastery of the Greek style, the pose and the nude body of the central figure resembling a Greek statue. An attendant with a classic profile patiently holds a mirror. *Boy Leading a Horse* (1905 or 1906), done in muted shades of blue, pink, terracotta, and gray, also suggests classical style. Both horse and boy resemble Greek statues, but unlike the woman in *La Toilette*, these figures seem to move. The boy walks

confidently and leads the horse with only the gesture of his hand.

Throughout the years from 1899 to 1905, Picasso continued to doubt himself and question his work, anxiously trying to find his own way of painting. Poor and inconvenienced by meager conditions and scant supplies, he felt isolated and alienated. Fernande thought of him as always uneasy and always seeking, but she did not know how seldom Picasso felt satisfied with his work. Fifteenth-century Italian painter Leonardo da Vinci said, "The painter who has no doubts makes little progress."[16] During those developing years Picasso had plenty of doubts.

3 Cubism: A New Art Form, 1905–1912

In the fall of 1905 Picasso still lived in Montmartre, a village built on a steep hill near the heart of Paris, where painters, writers, quiet citizens, and a few toughs went about their business without the crowds of tourists that visit the area today. Gradually chance events began to increase the sale of Picasso's paintings. And gradually his exposure to other artists' works helped him develop a new style of painting.

In November Picasso met Americans Leo and Gertrude Stein, a brother and sister who collected art. They bought his *Girl with a Basket of Flowers* and hung it with their paintings by Cézanne, Gauguin, and Matisse. They visited Picasso's studio and bought more pictures. This was the start of a long friendship. They hung his pictures in their flat, making his name known to their wide circle of friends; parties at their home introduced him to other buyers and to the French artist Henri Matisse.

Matisse brought two wealthy Russian buyers—Sergei Shchukine and Ivan Morosov—to Picasso's studio. Both bought many Picasso paintings over the years; their collections now hang in Moscow's Pushkin Museum. These sales prompted dealer Ambroise Vollard, another friend of the Steins, to buy thirty pictures for two thousand francs, an amount greater than any Picasso had ever had at one time. After years of poverty, Picasso finally had money, which he liked having, but hated getting. He hated bargaining with buyers about prices, and he hated parting with his pictures.

Growing Success

The paintings from the Pink Period and those inspired by Greek statues had brought him his first success. For a man with many self-doubts, this growing success was important. Years later, Picasso reflected on it, as reported by his friend, photographer Brassaï:

Success is an important thing! It has often been said that an artist should work for himself, for the love of art, and scorn success. It's a false idea. An artist needs success. Not only in order to live, but primarily so that he can realize his work. Even a rich painter should know success. Few people understand much about art, and not everyone is sensitive to painting. The majority judges a work of art in relation to its success. . . . But where is it written that success must always go to those who flatter the public taste? For myself, I wanted to prove that success can be obtained without compromise, even in opposition to all of the prevailing doctrines.[17]

Importance of Ancient and Contemporary Art

Early in 1906 Picasso was still thinking about ways to represent mass and volume on a flat surface. At the Louvre an exhibition of Iberian and pre-Roman sculptures of squat, heavy figures dating from 400–200 B.C., further inspired his curiosity. During this time Picasso asked to paint

Painted after attending an exhibition of Iberian sculptures, Portrait of Gertrude Stein *is reminiscent of the squat, heavy figures Picasso was fond of painting.*

Gertrude Stein because he was fascinated with her squat appearance. She sat eighty or ninety times for him as he worked with color and composition to depict her heaviness. Without finishing, he wiped out the face and went with Fernande to Gósol, a primitive village near Horta de Ebro in Catalonia.

In Gósol for the summer, Picasso sought isolation because he wanted to break from the kind of paintings he had done in Montmartre. His pictures of Fernande represent a new female. Picasso used contours alone, but no light, to emphasize her three-dimensional form. The figures are heavy and squat, painted in ochers—oranges and yellows—unlike the pink tones of the classical figure in *La Toilette.* By late summer his female figures had firmer contours and looked like sculptures. The faces looked like masks. These features suggest the influence of the Iberian sculptures. When he returned from Gósol, he painted the face of Gertrude Stein without seeing her; it is masklike with severe, asymmetric eyes, different in style from the rest of the painting. Picasso had become less interested in portraying a figure's outward appearance and more interested in capturing inner qualities.

Still perplexed about the best way to express space and volume and the most authentic colors to use, he studied past and contemporary art. He studied the Fauves, a word originally meaning "wild beasts," artists that included Matisse, Braque, and Dufy. The Fauves distorted the outlines of figures and used flat, bold patterns and bright colors. In 1906 Picasso attended an exhibition of Fauves, which featured Matisse's work *Joie de Vivre.* Though Picasso never joined the Fauves, he wanted to answer Matisse with a work of his own.

Picasso also studied the work of Cézanne, who created solid, enduring objects that portrayed strength and weight. To create this impression Cézanne made geometric shapes with lines and angles, giving the impression of depth. Cézanne said, "You must see in nature the cylinder, the sphere and the cone," identify light and dark places, and distort perspective. About Cézanne, Picasso told Brassaï: "He was my one and only master! Don't you think I looked at his pictures? I spent years studying them. . . . Cézanne! It was the same with all of us—he was like our father."[18]

In June 1907 Picasso had a startling experience at the Paris Musée de Sculpture Comparée. There he saw African sculptures in a gallery, or room, called the Musée d'Ethnographie. In that room Picasso also saw dolls, dummies, and primitive masks from the Ivory Coast and French Congo in Africa and New Caledonia in the South Pacific. Staring at those masks, he had a revelation, an emotional moment of knowledge, in which he felt in tune with the makers of the masks. Mask makers believed deeply in the masks' magical power to keep bad spirits away. Picasso realized that he, too, felt the need to keep away hostile forces, the internal forces that made him feel often like an outsider.

Invention of a New Art Form

These many influences finally came together in a painting Picasso worked on from early in 1907 through July. After filling seven sketchbooks and doing seventeen studies in preparation, he painted *Les Demoiselles d'Avignon* on a canvas 8 feet by 7 feet 8 inches. Although it is considered the first Cubist painting, art critic Alfred H. Barr Jr. says that it "is a transitional picture, a laboratory or, better, a battlefield of trial and experiment; but it is also a work of formidable, dynamic power unsurpassed in European art of its time."[19] The

Called "a battlefield of trial and experiment," Les Demoiselles d'Avignon, *painted in 1907, was Picasso's first painting in the Cubist style.*

nudes in this painting are women of a bordello on Avignon, a street in Barcelona. The space of the painting is broken up into angular wedges, or facets, curved to look either concave or convex. Like the sculptured women done in Gósol, the faces in *Les Demoiselles* look like masks. Unlike the Gósol figures, painted with curves to represent volume, these women are painted in straight lines and flat overlapping planes, or surfaces, making the women seem almost weightless.

A Revelation in a Museum

In Picasso: Pablo Ruiz Picasso: A Biography, *Patrick O'Brian quotes Picasso's explanation of the revelation he experienced with the African masks in the Musée d'Ethnographie.*

"I was all by myself. I wanted to get out. I didn't go: I stayed. It came to me that this was very important: something was happening to me, right?

Those masks were not just pieces of sculpture like the rest. Not in the least. They were magic. . . . These Negroes were intercessors [go-betweens]. . . . Against everything; against unknown, threatening spirits. I kept on staring at these fetishes. Then it came to me—I too felt that everything was unknown, hostile! Everything! Not just this and that but everything, women, children, animals, smoking, playing. . . . Everything! I understood what their sculpture meant to the blacks, what it was really for. Why carve like that and not in any other way? . . . All these fetishes were for the same thing. They were weapons. To help people not to be ruled by spirits anymore, to be independent. Tools. If you give spirits a shape, you break free from them. Spirits and the subconscious . . . and emotion—they're all the same thing. I grasped why I was a painter. All alone in that museum, surrounded by masks, Red Indian dolls, dummies covered with dust. The *Demoiselles* must have come that day: not at all because of their forms, no; but because it was my first exorcizing [freeing] picture—that's the point."

Picasso collected many sculptures from New Caledonia in his Bateau-Lavoir studio. The influence of Primitivism is evident in his works during this period.

Because of the differences between the left side of the canvas, which reflects colors and figures from Picasso's past work, and the right side of the canvas, which anticipates techniques he was working toward, the painting is significant as a transitional picture. On the left are three angular distortions of classical figures; on the right are two angular distortions of primitive figures. For the left side, Picasso used tans, pinks, and terracotta; for the right side he used gray, blues, and greens, with orange accents. The heads of the three figures on the left are less distorted, although the woman on the far left has an eye drawn in frontal view on a profile face and the central two women have noses drawn in profile on frontal faces. The heads of the two figures on the right reveal the most radical differences between the two sides. Alfred H. Barr Jr. describes them:

> The upper head is no longer flat but foreshortened, with a flat-ridged nose, a sharp chin, a small oval mouth and deleted ears, all characteristic of certain African Negro masks of the French Congo. . . . In the face below the tentative three-dimensional foreshortening of the upper and doubtless earlier head gives way to a flattened mask in which eyes, nose, mouth and ear are distorted or even dislocated. The hand and arm which support this lower head are even more violently distorted. Like their forms, the coloring and hatched shading of these two faces seem inspired in a general way by the masks of the Congo or Ivory Coast.[20]

Picasso used hatching, fine parallel lines, to make shadows and to create tension. A basket of fruit near the center and bottom unites the two sides.

A Shocked Reaction

Les Demoiselles shocked Picasso's artist friends. Matisse thought the painting was a hoax designed to discredit modern art. Writer André Salmon thought Picasso had abandoned his fellow artists and was losing his grip on the new style of painting developed by the Fauves. Picasso biographer O'Brian quotes the words of Leo Stein, who said, "You have been trying to paint the fourth dimension; how amusing," and Ambroise Vollard, who said, "It's the work of a madman."[21] Picasso was hurt and discouraged by their comments and put the painting aside for ten years. However, he went on painting postscripts to *Les Demoiselles* for months after. Biographer Pierre Daix explains the shocked reaction this way:

> What was so disconcerting and scandalizing about *Les Demoiselles d'Avignon* was not so much this technical revolution as the fact that Picasso had attacked the human figure itself and discarded the conventional representation of man made in the image and likeness of God.[22]

Late in 1907 Picasso met Georges Braque, who was also interested in new techniques to represent volume on a canvas. After seeing *Les Demoiselles*, Braque said, "To paint in such a way was as bad as drinking petrol [gasoline] in the hope of spitting fire."[23] Though he was shocked, Braque recognized Picasso's revolutionary ideas and said that the painting moved him as no painting had before. Within a short time the two men shared ideas and techniques and discussed each other's work.

Inspired by primitive African masks, Picasso created this sculpture of Fernande using sharp angles and geometric shapes.

In the meantime, Picasso worked on sculpture, in a style inspired by the African masks. In 1908 he did a sculpture of Fernande using wedges to create a rigid, elongated nose, lips pursed outward, and eyes reduced nearly to geometric forms. Critics identify these works as the Negro Period. Picasso denied ever creating "Negro art," but the identification remains as a reference point in the history of Picasso's work.

New Places to Work

Throughout Picasso's life changes in his art accompanied changes in the locations where he worked. In September 1909 he moved from the Bateau-Lavoir to 11 Boulevard de Clichy, at the foot of Butte Montmartre. The new flat had a studio and several rooms, which Picasso furnished with oak, mahogany, and brass furniture. His friends—Guillaume Apollinaire, the Steins, Matisse, Max Jacob, Braque—gathered for dinners served by a maid in a starched apron. But his studio filled up with old furniture, musical instruments, and African masks, giving it a slumlike appearance that seemed to relax Picasso. After three years he moved to Boulevard Raspail. Each move in his life required increasingly more work because Picasso loved to collect but hated to part with anything.

Summers usually found Picasso in new places. In 1908 he went to a village north of Paris, in 1909 back to Horta de Ebro, in 1910 to Cadaqués on the Mediterranean coast of Spain, and in 1911 to Cerét in southern France. Each trip involved the transportation of his personal things, his big dog Frika, his pet monkey, his painting supplies, and, until 1912, Fernande. Frequently his friends moved too; during these summers his painting colleague Braque often worked nearby. More than just a restless person, Picasso loved the sun and warmth near the Mediterranean. They gave him health, and the new scenery gave him subjects for his pictures.

Picasso's relationship with Fernande became gradually more strained after the move to the flat on de Clichy and ended in the spring of 1912. By that time Picasso had met Marcelle Humbert, a gentle, delicate woman whom Picasso called Eve or Eva. After she became his companion, Picasso included in some of his paintings his pet name for Eva, taken from the words of a popular song, *Ma Jolie* ("my pretty one"). Picasso and Eva were companions until she died four years later.

The first decade of the twentieth century had established Picasso as a successful artist. By the time he was twenty-five years old, he had produced many hundreds of drawings and more than two hundred paintings, more paintings than many artists do in a lifetime. Furthermore, he had become an engraver and a watercolor painter, and he had learned sculpture, each medium handled with equal skill. Daniel-Henry Kahnweiler had become the exclusive dealer of Picasso works, an arrangement and friendship that lasted more than sixteen years. Germans, Russians, Hungarians, and even Chinese bought his works. Picasso's future seemed secure.

New Challenges and New Forms

The 1907 *Les Demoiselles d'Avignon* had been but a step toward the solution to an art problem that haunted Picasso. While many people thought of painting as an art concerned with a story, social messages, or effects of light on objects, Picasso focused on the problem of form. He had posed two questions for himself: How can I express volume and make a three-dimensional reconstruction of reality on the flat surface of a canvas in a new way? and, How can I portray different views of a given object and merge them into a single image on a flat surface? For answers Picasso returned to the instruction of Cézanne, who had urged the use of the cylinder, the

Cézanne, who painted La Montagne Sainte-Victoire, *influenced Picasso in the use of the cylinder, the sphere, and the cone to make a three-dimensional reconstruction of reality on a flat canvas.*

The Artist's Mystery

In Picasso on Art, *Dore Ashton quotes Picasso's explanation of the mysterious quality that a great painting has.*

"Something holy, that's it. . . . It's a word something like that [holy] we should be able to use, but people would take it in the wrong way. You ought to be able to say that a painting is as it is, with its capacity to move us, because it is as though it were touched by God. But people would think it a sham. And yet that is what's nearest to the truth.

No explanation can be given in words. Except that by some liaison between the man-creator and what is highest in the human spirit, something happens which gives this power to the painted reality.

You can search for a thousand years , and you will find nothing. Everything can be explained scientifically today. Except that [painting]. You can go to the moon or walk under the sea, or anything else you like, but painting remains painting because it eludes such investigation. It remains there like a question. And it alone gives the answer.

It has that good fortune. And that misfortune. And we too."

sphere, and the cone. But Cézanne had never mentioned the prism or the cube. Picasso and Braque began almost where Cézanne left off. They abandoned bright color and used tan and dun gray. They analyzed natural shapes and then re-created them into geometric shapes. Out of the fragments, they tried to convey the spirit, not the appearance, of objects and figures. Yet Picasso always retained a hint of the original object, creating a link between the reality of the object and the reality of its portrayal on the canvas.

Both Picasso and Braque worked on these problems in 1909. When artist Louis Vauxcelles saw Braque's exhibition of cubist paintings, he said that Braque "despises form and reduces everything—views, places, people, houses—to geometrical diagrams, to cubes."[24] The word *cube* caught on, and Cubism became the name for the new style of painting the two artists had developed. Because they analyzed shapes, the method was also called Analytic Cubism.

Picasso's Cubist paintings between 1909 and 1912 show a progression from larger to smaller shapes, from color to shades of gray and tan, and from more- to less-identifiable subjects. In *Factory at Horta de Ebro* (1909) the trees, chimney, mountains, and buildings are easily recognizable,

The prismlike design of Ma Jolie *(1911–1912), with its small geometric planes and great distortion, is characteristic of High Analytic Cubism.*

as are the cylinders, spheres, cones, and cubes. A more advanced stage of Picasso's Cubism, *Woman with Pears* (1909) has small, angular shapes for the eyes, nose, and mouth and presents a front view of Fernande's face and a side view of her neck. Picasso used green for the background, soft red for fruit and a table, and ocher and gray for the woman's face and shoulders. (Fernande disliked all cubist paintings of her because she thought they made her look old.)

Girl with a Mandolin (1910)—unfinished because the model, Fanny Tellier, became impatient and quit—is a transi-

tion piece, as Picasso moved toward smaller geometric shapes. The shapes are flatter in appearance and are graduated more finely than those in the paintings of Fernande. The differences produce a softer effect. In spite of the geometric distortions, the girl and her mandolin are easily identifiable.

High Analytic Cubism

After painting *Girl with a Mandolin*, Picasso did a series of portraits of his friends Vollard, Kahnweiler, and Uhde, all in a similar style. These paintings are called High, or abstract, Analytic Cubism because they have small geometric planes, many of them prisms. The luminous and often transparent facets, or shapes, tend to reflect back upon themselves to give another layer of depth. Distortion is greater, and the color is more neutral. In spite of the distortion, each portrait conveys the man's personality.

After these portraits, Picasso's High Analytic Cubism became even more abstract. He painted still lifes, heads, and people with musical instruments in a style that is difficult to read. (To read a painting, the viewer must consider a picture as a picture, separate from its subject, and see its harmonies and arrangement of objects.) These paintings have planes, lines, shading, and space, but those features no longer describe, or set off, the subjects. Barr reports Picasso as saying, "Cubism is an art dealing primarily with forms."[25] These paintings have no sculptural relief to help identify the subject. They have flat, shaded planes, which mostly obscure the subject. The light in the early Cubist paint-

An Opinion of Cubism

The sculptor Manolo, one of the members of the Els Quatre Gats group and a friend of Picasso, expressed his opinion of Picasso's Cubism, which Marilyn McCully quotes in A Picasso Anthology: Documents, Criticism, Reminiscences.

"I saw the birth and death of many literary and artistic schools, and I saw many fashions go by, expiring soon after their much vaunted first appearance. In Picasso's studio I witnessed the birth of Cubism. If my memory does not fail me, Picasso used to talk a lot then about the fourth dimension and he carried around the mathematics books of Henri Poincaré. Cubism, to be honest, I have never understood and I do not know what it is. Looking at one of the earliest cubist portraits of Picasso's I asked him what he would say if the next day— let us suppose—when he went to the railway station to welcome his mother, she appeared in the form of a cubist figure. At any rate, Picasso is such a great painter that he is good even doing Cubism, and he is a thousand kilometres ahead of his imitators and camp followers."

ings illuminated the subject from the outside and helped the viewer see it. The light in the late Cubist paintings appears to come from within the objects that Picasso has disassembled. In these, light seems to symbolize the mind, inviting the viewer to enter the mind too.

Ma Jolie (*Woman with a Zither or Guitar*) (1911–1912) illustrates features of this phase of Analytic Cubism. With only a slight tie to external reality, the painting is as abstract as Picasso's work ever became. With study, a viewer could probably see a human figure, but the subtitle helps the viewer know what to look for. Art historian and curator William Rubin guides the viewer's search:

The sitter's head . . . can be made out at the top center of the composition;

her left arm is bent at the elbow—perhaps resting on the arm of a chair . . . and her hand probably holds the bottom of a guitar whose vertical strings are visible in the center. Together with the wine glass at the left and the treble clef and musical staff at the bottom of the picture, all this suggests an ambience of informal music-making.[26]

Picasso's most abstract paintings, such as this one, can be reproduced in photographs with only partial success. Standing before an original work and concentrating on it, a viewer sees more than a photograph reveals. In the original, the light is more luminous, the perspective is deeper, and the subject gradually moves into view.

With this last phase of Analytic Cubism, Picasso carried his break with reality to the extreme, and the public and the critics sent up an outcry. People at exhibitions reacted with anger or laughter. Some said Picasso was guilty of creating hideous, outrageous art and called his paintings horrors. One journal said that the novelty of the pictures was a return to barbarism, that the paintings were primitive and savage and an insult to what was beautiful in life and nature. André Salmon pointed out that Picasso had invented Cubism after long discussions with philosophers, poets, and mathematicians. At first, Salmon thought Picasso harmless when he "laid the first stone, the first cube," but later he thought Picasso's work was not praiseworthy. Another critic called Cubism "self-satisfied ignorance." When an American audience first saw a collection of Cubist drawings and prints, viewers thought one of Picasso's nudes was a fire escape.

Not all, however, reacted with outrage. One critic pointed out that the Cubist planes "slide" into a new order of art, a new way of organizing reality. Many painters saw Cubism "as a most radical and convincing break from the past . . .

and as a living hope for the future."[27] Many artists became Cubist painters and exhibited their works in greater numbers at Paris art shows. While the public and the critics were attacking Picasso and his Cubist works, his fame grew, spreading fast to influential, though small, circles in Paris, Germany, and Russia.

When Picasso went among the public, people asked him to explain his paintings. They asked, What do they mean? As author Dore Ashton reports, Picasso told a friend:

Everyone wants to understand art. Why not try to understand the songs of a bird? Why does one love the night, flowers, everything around one, without trying to understand them? But in the case of a painting people have to *understand*. If only they would realize above all that an artist works [out] of necessity, that he himself is only a trifling bit of the world, and that no more importance should be attached to him than to plenty of other things which please us in the world, though we can't explain them.[28]

4 Collages, Ballet, and a Turning Point, 1912–1922

By 1912 Cubism had become an art movement in Paris, but the public still jeered at it. Consequently, Cubists, who considered Picasso their leader, banded together and socialized away from public criticism. Writer and art critic Guillaume Apollinaire, who supported the Cubists, edited a magazine called *The Cubist Painters*. After he had published some of Picasso's Cubist drawings, the public criticism was so intense that he had to resign. Picasso, however, remained independent and continued to focus on Analytic Cubism and to work on a new idea—introducing actual objects into his paintings.

Synthetic Cubism

The years from 1912 through mid-1914 brought a quieter life to Picasso and Eva, his new companion. They spent three summers in Cerét, France, near the Spanish border, where Picasso worked hard and often discussed new techniques with Cubists Georges Braque and Juan Gris. During the summer of 1913 Picasso's father died in Barcelona, but Picasso did not attend the funeral even though he was only a hundred miles away. He gave no explanation, but Eva was ill with tuberculosis at the time.

Early in 1912 Picasso still painted in the style of Analytic Cubism, but he also experimented with his new idea. Working together at the time, Picasso and Braque both introduced actual objects into their paintings: Braque a real nail and Picasso letters of the alphabet. Using objects was the beginning of Synthetic Cubism. Picasso and Braque reasoned that because canvas and paint are mere objects, then, logically, they could be replace by other objects. They imagined replacing paint by cutting out colored, textured objects and glueing them onto the canvas. They could unify these separate pieces with lines and paint. The name Synthetic Cubism came from the word *synthesize*, meaning to combine in order to form a new and complex product. The new works were called collages, a word derived from the French *coller*, to glue. By definition, a collage is an artistic composition of different materials glued onto a surface, and Picasso unified the pieces with lines.

One of the first examples of Synthetic Cubism was Picasso's *Still Life with Chair Caning* (1912), a collage made with rope, letters cut from a newspaper, and a piece of oilcloth, printed to look like chair caning. Pasted onto the canvas, the oilcloth represents a chair, but it is an imitation of a chair seat at the same time that it is a

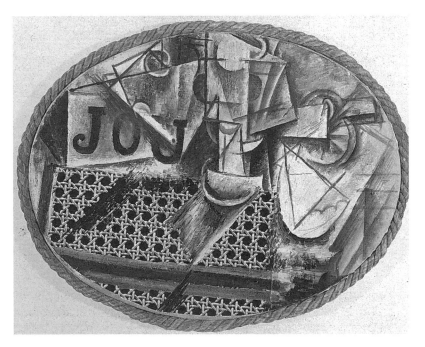

Representing Synthetic Cubism, Still Life with Chair Caning *incorporates actual objects into the painting. This revolutionary collage combines painted and real objects, yet retains a Cubist point of view.*

piece of real oilcloth. Although this painting is revolutionary for its combination of paint and real objects, it is also a Cubist work because the space is flat, but the objects appear from different angles instead of a single, traditional point of view. For example, a person sitting and looking at a glass and a knife on a table sees them from one angle, but if the person stands up and looks down at the glass and knife, they look different. The seated or standing person can imagine what the glass and knife would look like from the other position. A Cubist work portrays both angles and possibly several others.

Each of Picasso's Cubist paintings depicts objects from at least two points of view. In *Still Life with Chair Caning,* a pipe is in perspective but a bowl is a white circle as if it were viewed from above. Hélène Seckel, curator of the Musée Picasso, explains that even though objects appear from different points of view,

these objects remain recognizable just the same: pipe, newspaper . . . stemmed glass, lemon slice, knife, scallop shell, these all seem to have been placed on the caned chair or on a table that apparently coincides with the oval of the canvas itself. As a final whimsical touch, Picasso used a real piece of rope to frame the picture, an allusion to the ornamental trim used on tablecloths to fit them around the top of the table.[29]

In this picture Picasso juggled reality and point of view: what seems to be most real, the oilcloth, is the most false; what seems most abstract, the distorted pieces, are all recognizable objects seen in local cafés.

In the collages made from 1912 to 1914, Picasso used string, glass, sand, tobacco packages, bottle labels, nails, wood, and pieces of fabric. For many Synthetic Cubist works, he used only paper combined with paint and charcoal. Called *papier collé* (pasted paper), the technique involved layering shapes of paper, some for the background and others to make objects and shadows.

For example, *Student with a Pipe* (1913–1914) combines oil, charcoal, sand, and pasted paper. Picasso cut out a paper beret, colored it dark reddish brown, painted on details for the headband and the clip, and then crumpled the paper to make it stand out in relief. He contoured the student's cheeks with charcoal and used a large blue-gray rectangle on the left for the shadow made by the head. The flat ears have wavy lines, repeated in the hair. A black dot, representing the opening of the figure's left ear, stands between tiny

Exemplary of the papier collé *technique,* Student with a Pipe *displays a paper beret pasted on the canvas and enhanced with paint.*

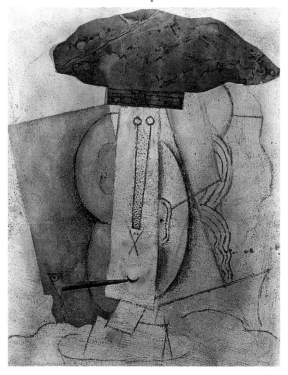

dots that represent nostrils and little circles that make eyes. A dot and a circle also make the top of the tobacco-pipe bowl. Stippled (painted with dots), the long nose suggests the same texture as that of the overall surface, which is sprinkled with grains of sand. Picasso's humor enlivens these simple lines and ordinary materials, as if he were making a joke of Cubism.

The Disruption of War

Picasso's and Braque's Cubist work stopped when World War I broke out in 1914. Jean Leymarie reports Picasso's comment: "On 2 August 1914 I took Braque and Derain to the [train] station in Avignon. I never saw them again. . . . The cubist movement as such was now at an end and henceforth each artist followed a path of his own."[30]

The French may have been excited and patriotic, but for Spanish-born Picasso, the war brought personal unhappiness and total disruption of his daily life. His artist friends had gone to war, and the Steins and his German art dealer, Kahnweiler, had left Paris. Few people felt like buying art. Two German art critics had supported Cubism, but because Germans were now considered enemies, their support convinced some French people that Cubist painting was unpatriotic and that Picasso was suspect. Again Picasso was an outsider; he was, as O'Brian says, "the remote spectator of a quarrel that was not his own."[31]

Picasso's sadness and alienation continued through the year. By the fall of 1915 Eva's tuberculosis had worsened, and Picasso took her to the hospital, where she died during the winter. Saddened by Eva's death, Picasso wrote to Gertrude Stein: "My poor Eva is dead . . . a great sorrow . . . she was always so kind to me."[32] Picasso fled the studio at rue Schoelcher, where they had lived, and withdrew into a small, suburban house in Montrouge, his first effort at living alone. His work did not stop, but 1915 was one of the least-productive years in his life.

During this period Picasso wanted to see if he could still draw, "like everybody else," the kind of drawings his father had taught him. As a test he made pencil portraits of his friends Jacob, Vollard, and Apollinaire. He drew with precision, giving their features detail and their clothing texture and shadows as he had drawn the La Coruña beggars. Biographers Frank Elgar and Robert Maillard said that "these portraits are sheer masterpieces of which even the most realistic painter might be proud, . . . [showing] deep respect for natural forms."[33] But the drawings caused an uproar among other Cubists, who were outraged that their leader had shifted to realism. Biographer Pierre Daix said, "It was perhaps easier to break with five hundred years of Western painting than to affront the Cubists, who claimed him as their own and who would certainly feel abandoned in adversity."[34]

What Is Art?

Many non-Cubist viewers, on the other hand, wondered why Picasso painted a Cubist portrait of Vollard, for example, when he could draw a realistic portrait of him.

London Newspapers Attack Cubism

In 1921 Leicester Galleries in London exhibited seventy-two Picasso pictures, some of which were collages. In Picasso, *Patrick O'Brian quotes how the right-wing press and scandal sheets reviewed Cubist works.*

Morning Post: "It has been said that Pablo Picasso's art has a logic of its own like that of music. What sort of music? The caterwauling love songs of cats in the night? That is the only kind of music suggested by Picasso's cubist diagrams at the Leicester Galleries."

Daily Mail: "[The work is] a Cubist conception of a packet of tobacco by Pablo Picasso, arch-apostle of this extraordinary art. We are not sure, however, if this is the right way up."

Sketch: "To draw a few triangles and a segment of a circle, colour them crudely, stick some patches of cement with sand in it and call the whole 'Nature Morte' smacks of idiocy."

Proving that he could still draw with accuracy and detail, Picasso created this portrait (right) of Ambroise Vollard in 1915. Unlike his earlier Cubist rendition (left), this portrait focused on textures, shadows, and the features of Vollard rather than geometric planes or distortion.

This attitude implies that pictures with greater realism are better art. Such speculation relates to basic questions that Picasso had struggled with from his days at Els Quatre Gats in Barcelona. What is art? What is the artist's purpose? Defining and measuring art is difficult. Picasso wanted to solve the problem of representing a new reality suitable for his own time. And he was determined to rely on his own judgment. The history of art shows what has been good art, and Picasso repeatedly turned to the past for guidance, but never to imitate any style.

In *History of Art,* H. W. Janson explains what distinguishes an artist from an artisan, or craftsman. First, an artist, Janson says, resists rules, which Picasso certainly did, while an artisan requires them. Second, an artist never knows for certain how a picture will turn out, as if he or she were in a game of seeking and finding, whereas an artisan knows what he or she is trying to imitate. Picasso told a friend, "I never do a painting as a work of art. All of them

are researches. I search incessantly."[35] Third, an artist assumes that the hand will be able to execute what the imagination sees, whereas an artisan tries to execute what the eye sees. Since painting a picture consists of many imaginative leaps, the hand must form and shape the material as the imagination visualizes. Picasso said: "I don't know in advance what I am going to put on canvas any more than I decide beforehand what colors I am going to use."[36] Unless the artist's hand is skilled, it is unable to create what the imagination conceives. Picasso said: "The brushstroke itself is a creative art."[37]

Fourth, according to Janson, "Even the most painstaking piece of craft does not deserve to be called a work of art unless it involves a leap of the imagination."[38] Therefore, lacking imagination, neither a computer nor an artisan makes art. What sets the artist apart is "that mysterious ability to *find* which we call talent, not to be confused with aptitude which the craftsman has."[39] Picasso's art resulted from his imagination, skill, and mysterious ability to find his own truth and beauty.

Ballet and a Dancer

After his difficult time in 1915 and 1916, Picasso's neighbor, a composer named Erik Satie, introduced Picasso to Jean Cocteau, who was producing a ballet. Cocteau persuaded Picasso to make sets and costumes. In 1917 Picasso and Cocteau went to Rome to join Sergey Diaghilev and his Russian ballet company to prepare for *Parade*, a Cubist ballet. The company returned to Paris for the opening in May 1917, and the ballet enraged the audience. O'Brian writes:

> The anger of the bourgeois who had paid to see a ballet and who were being shown Cubism in motion to the sound of typewriters grew louder and louder; . . . toward the end the whole theatre was filled with shrieks and catcalls, howls of disapprobating [disapproving], malevolent [malicious] hissing and boos, . . . but it was not a real failure either. . . . The brighter members of the audience . . . had been entranced; and when it was produced again in Paris after the war it was in fact recognized as a brilliant manifestation of the new spirit.[40]

While in Rome preparing for the ballet, Picasso had met Olga Kaklova, a minor dancer in the company. She became Picasso's companion when they returned to Paris. After performances there the ballet company began a tour in Spain and South America. To be with Olga, Picasso followed the company to Barcelona, where he

While designing ballet sets and costumes, Picasso met Olga Kaklova. One of his first portraits of Kaklova is pictured.

painted Olga wearing a mantilla, the first of many portraits of her. When the company continued its tour to South America, Olga quit dancing and returned to Paris with Picasso. In August 1918 they married at the cathedral of St. Alexander Nevsky.

Marriage brought changes to Picasso's life. Supposedly the daughter of a Russian noble, Olga was used to high-class living. The couple chose a two-story flat on rue de la Boëtie, a quiet, grand street near the Champs Élysées, and they socialized with dancers, musicians, and theater people. Picasso and Olga attended opening performances and receptions and dressed in formal clothes. Picasso's friend Sabartés joked when he saw Picasso in a bow tie and a breast-pocket handkerchief, "The attention he pays to his appearance is unbelievable."[41]

Between 1918 and 1920, Picasso designed sets and costumes for five more ballets. Then the birth of a child shifted his attention. On February 4, 1921, Picasso and Olga's son Paulo was born. The child brought delight and goodwill to Picasso, who thought of his son as "a fascinating object, earthy, genuine, timeless, peculiarly his own, and one that he drew again and again," according to biographer O'Brian.[42] The baby inspired Picasso to do a series of pictures with a mother and a child—maternities, they were called.

A Turning Point

During the years leading up to and following 1920, Picasso's art reached a turning point. Not yet forty years old, he had already revolutionized art with Cubism. He had experimented for a time with realistic drawing. He had returned to his artistic roots for guidance, to the classical art of ancient Greece and Rome. Out of these different directions, he developed something new. He was able to work in both classical and modern styles at the same time, imaginatively blending elements from each. Discovering this blend of styles marked a turning point in his artistic career.

Three works illustrate how this change evolved, and each one illustrates how he blended two styles. First, Picasso summed up his Cubist work in two large canvases in which he presented two versions of the same subject, both titled *Three Musicians* (1921). These two works combined Analytic and Synthetic Cubism. In one, masked figures of a Pierrot and a Harlequin sit behind a table and play a recorder and a guitar while a monk sings. A dog lies at their feet. In the other, Picasso changed the figures' positions and instruments, excluded the dog and used lighter colors. He painted both as if he had cut out colored paper and glued the designs onto the surface, thereby blending collage Cubism with painting.

Seated Woman (1920) blends classical art with distortion. The figure sits in the pose of a draped Greek statue, but Picasso's seated woman is a giantess with huge, deformed hands and feet, her size heightened by contrasts of light and shadow. Third, Picasso combined classical and Cubist forms. *Bathers* (1918) on one hand, alludes to classical Greek vase painting and antique statues. On the other hand, as Hélène Seckel points out,

Seated Woman *combines classical form with modern distortion.*

In Bathers, *Picasso blends classical Greek forms and a Cubist perspective. This meshing of different styles symbolized a turning point in Picasso's artistic career.*

the "bather in the striped swimsuit has been represented simultaneously with front and back views, proof of the lasting effects of Cubism's effort to show things from all different angles."[43]

Following this turning point Picasso blended styles and developed new ones, choosing the best variation for his subject. About his own style, according to Ashton, Picasso said:

Basically I am perhaps a painter without style. Style is often something which locks the painter into the same vision, the same technique, the same formula during years and years, sometimes during one's whole lifetime. One recognizes it immediately, but it's always the same suit, or the same cut of the suit. There are, nevertheless, great painters with style. I myself thrash around too much. You see me here and yet I'm already changed. I'm already elsewhere. I'm never fixed and that's why I have no style.[44]

5 Post-Cubism Picasso, 1922–1936

Picasso had established his place in art by age thirty-three and had revolutionized it by age forty. Another person might have retired then, but not Picasso. After the turning point, he seemed to have a new freedom, and he tried a variety of new forms. Looking for a pattern, art historians puzzled about how Picasso's art was evolving and often asked him. Impatient with the questions, reports biographer O'Brian, Picasso told Marius de Zayas:

> Repeatedly I am asked to explain how my painting evolved. To me there is no past or future in art. . . . Variation does not mean evolution. If an artist varies his mode of expression this only means that he has changed his manner of thinking.[45]

During the early 1920s Picasso's painting reflected the joy he felt in his family. For example, *Woman in White* (1923) portrays another classical, seated woman. Instead of the huge hands and heaviness of the women painted three years earlier, this woman with delicate features sits in a chair, relaxed, wearing a white dress. Moreover, Picasso often painted his son, as in *Paulo as Harlequin* (1924). He portrayed his son with idyllic innocence and dark, piercing eyes like his own. The Harlequin in blue and yellow sits on a black chair;

the feet of both child and chair are unfinished, giving a sense that they float on the surface of the canvas.

In Paulo as Harlequin, *Picasso portrays his son with softness and innocence. These joyful qualities are reflected in many of his paintings during the early 1920s.*

Picasso wanted his possessions in his studio left untouched, dust and all. In Picasso, *Wilhelm Boeck and Jaime Sabartés explain the importance of the cluttered environment.*

"But in the course of his daily life nothing upsets him. That there are mountains of books on the floor does not matter a bit. Papers everywhere and a thousand things in his way? He does not care. What does matter is that everything forever remain just where he left it so that his eyes may find rest in an unchanging environment. It is a visual necessity that no change should surprise him. . . . Thus he is the supreme conservative. He keeps all his possessions piled up around him. He does not part with anything."

New Techniques

During the twenties two familiar themes reappeared—bathers and still lifes before an open window—but with new techniques. In *Three Bathers* (1923) the women suggest Greek statues, but Picasso has both foreshortened and elongated their bodies. To foreshorten is to draw one body part proportionately shorter than the other parts; to elongate is to draw one body part proportionately longer than the others. For example, one of his women, running into the water, has an elongated outstretched leg and a foreshortened torso and head. With one foot on the beach, the woman gives the impression that her head stretches impossibly far out over the water. Here, Picasso has played with our familiar notions of time, the time it takes to cover a certain space.

In a 1924 still life, *The Red Tablecloth*, Picasso combined the tans and grays of past Cubist paintings with brilliant red. While most of the shapes for the window and table have straight lines and angles, the objects—a statue, fruit, and a mandolin—have curved lines. Picasso's use of curved lines and brilliant color pointed the direction toward a new kind of Cubism.

For many years Picasso's Cubist works had sold for higher prices than the works of other Cubist artists, and Picasso had improved his own skills at negotiating with buyers. Consequently, he became rich enough to buy a Hispano-Suiza, his first automobile. Since he never learned to drive, he hired a permanent chauffeur. Both car and chauffeur were the envy of other artists.

By 1925 Picasso had grown dissatisfied with his high-class way of life and particularly with his marriage to Olga. Besides being jealous and possessive, Olga appeared indifferent to Picasso and his work. She had plenty of servants and little to do, and she had a husband whose major interest was his work. Though Picasso could be a stubborn and inattentive companion, he also had a kind and generous nature and felt responsible to his family. But he was often careless about managing daily activities, a quality that irritated his wife. As family tension increased, Picasso felt his work affected—that it lacked the force it once had; art had to have energy to be good, he believed. Moreover, he found that violence and monster images had crept into his work.

Picasso's Surreal Paintings

Picasso's work began to resemble Surrealist paintings. Surrealists tried to paint what was in the unconscious mind; they painted as if they had closed their eyes and let a psychic force free what lay in the mind's depths. Their pictures had dreamlike qualities and symbols, and they portrayed the horrors and the joys hidden within. Surrealist painters, such as Salvador Dalí, Max Ernst, and Joan Miró, claimed that Picasso belonged to their movement. Though Picasso was interested in the Surrealists, he never became a true Surrealist because he was unable to approach the world with his eyes closed or to borrow from the hazy dreamworld. Picasso's images were his own conscious ones, emerging from personal discontent that grew as his marriage deteriorated.

Three works illustrate Picasso's Surrealist-like art. Max Ernst had done dot drawings that he called essays in automatic drawing; he began with random dots, hoping to produce an artistic expression. In 1926 Picasso filled a sketch book with groups of dots connected by lines. Most of the drawings are small and suggest a figure or a musical instrument, but one

larger work suggests a woman's face. Sixteen pages of Picasso's dot drawings later served as illustrations for a special edition of a book by the French writer Balzac. Another work, *Guitar* (1926) derives its Surrealist qualities from the emotion it suggests. Made from an apron, rake tines, string, paper, and nails, the work is simple and crude. A hole burned in the fabric and sharp ends of long rusty nails pointing outward suggest anger and violence, as if Picasso's deeply hidden emotions had emerged in the work.

Some critics thought *Three Dancers* (1925) was like Surrealist art because the distorted dancers and their wild frenzy suggest disquieting emotions. Others saw the painting as a skillful blend of Cubism and classical tradition. H. W. Janson explains:

> The two tracks of Picasso's style began to converge, making an extraordinary synthesis that has . . . become the basis of his art. The *Three Dancers* of 1925 shows how he accomplished this seemingly impossible feat. Structurally, the picture is pure collage Cubism; it even includes painted imitations of specific materials—patterned wallpaper, and samples of various fabrics cut out with pinking shears. But the figures, a wildly fantastic version of a classical scheme . . . are an even more violent assault on convention than the figures in the *Demoiselles d'Avignon*. Human anatomy is here simply the raw material for Picasso's incredibly fertile inventiveness; limbs, breasts, and faces are handled with . . . freedom. . . . Their original identity no longer matters—breasts turn into eyes, profiles merge with frontal views, shadows become substance.[46]

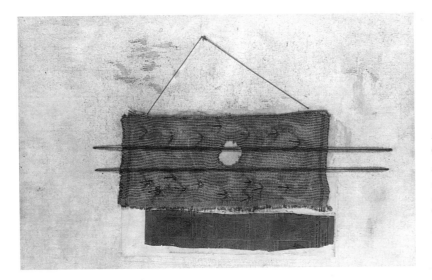

Resembling Surrealist works, Guitar (left) suggests Picasso's frustration with his deteriorating marriage. Often called surrealistic, Picasso's Three Dancers (below) combines collage Cubism, classical forms, and Greek mythology.

The "classical scheme" Janson refers to comes from Greek mythology. On Mount Olympus lived a band of three sisters, called the Three Graces: Splendor, Mirth, and Good Cheer. Together they represented grace and beauty. When they danced their enchanted dance to the accompaniment of Apollo's lyre, they delighted the gods and made a man happy. In Picasso's *Three Dancers* the blend of Cubism and classical mythology has several ironic elements. First, behind the right-hand dancer in Picasso's picture is the profile of a man, but it is dark and sober, not the face of one made happy by a visit from the Graces. Furthermore, Picasso's women, with their distorted faces and big feet, can hardly be called models of grace and beauty; they would not likely be named Splendor, Mirth, and Good Cheer. And, finally, while the Graces delighted the gods, Picasso's dancers produce an uneasy emotion in viewers.

Picasso carried distortion even further during the summers from 1927 to 1929 when he painted bathers again. Called metamorphoses or monsters by critics, these paintings portray nudes with bodies that contain human elements, but Picasso has rearranged the parts. These figures appear to be the opposite of beauty. The word *metamorphosis* means a transformation, a marked change in appearance. For example, *The Swimmer* (1929) seems to float without weight and has limbs stretching in all directions. One hand is about to break from the arm, and one foot is partially transparent. The swimmer is missing either her head or one of her limbs, unless Picasso intended that the lower right limb double as a head. The finger pointing, or perhaps the nose, has two dots that may be a pair of nostrils.

During the late 1920s Picasso's marriage to Olga was emotionally over. She resisted divorce, and Picasso, who knew nothing about divorce procedures, procrastinated, as he often did in practical matters. In the early part of 1927 he met seventeen-year-old Marie-Thérèse Walter in front of an art gallery. He told her he wanted to make her portrait because he thought her face interesting. Picasso's name meant nothing to her, but they began a relationship that lasted for ten years. A tall, fair-haired, athletic Swiss woman, she was calm and undemanding. Since he was still officially married to Olga, Picasso kept his relationship with Marie-Thérèse a secret, even from his friends, until she appeared in his paintings and sculptures in 1931.

New Kinds of Sculpture

In spite of the turmoil in his personal life, Picasso kept working and learned a new medium—metal sculpture. He learned how to weld iron and cast bronze. He did several versions of *Wire Construction* (1928). Formed of rods, empty spaces, and metal circles, these three-dimensional versions of his dot drawings made charming

Extending the limits of distortion, The Swimmer *is referred to as a metamorphosis. Although human elements exist, the swimmer's body parts have been rearranged and distorted to create a very unnatural effect.*

Wire Construction *is composed of rods and empty spaces that create a three-dimensional effect.*

figures. With sheet metal, wire, and metal scraps, he made *Woman in a Garden* (1929–1930). Sheet metal pieces formed the woman's face, blowing hair, and philodendron leaves. He assembled and welded the parts and painted the whole piece white. After he had learned to cast in bronze, he made figures from boxes, leaves, corrugated cardboard—whatever he found lying around—and then bronzed them. In 1934 he made *Woman with Leaves* and *Woman with an Orange.* Out of simple junk, he created these charming, innocent female figures.

In 1930 Picasso bought a large country house forty miles outside Paris. The Château de Boisgeloup had outbuildings, stables, and a coach house, all suitable as studios. The château was the perfect place for Picasso to work on sculptures. Besides his metal work and junk sculptures, he worked in traditional methods—clay and plaster molded on a wire armature, which is a framework that makes a supportive core to hold wet clay or plaster.

From the moment he had met Marie-Thérèse, Picasso visualized her in sculptures because he thought she had a fascinating head, forehead, and nose. Picasso made many white plaster heads and busts of Marie-Thérèse, some over 6 feet high, which his friend Brassaï photographed. He described how Picasso opened the door and "in all their brilliant whiteness we beheld a nation of sculptured figures."[47] Picasso sculpted Marie-Thérèse's unusual profile in a form like the head of a merino sheep. These busts, called simply *Head of a Woman* or *Bust of a Woman,* also have classical features that recall the beauty of ancient statues: the Greek profile, small mouth, and rounded chin. Because plaster is fragile, Picasso cast many sculptures in bronze, but he waited a long time because he liked their plaster whiteness.

Curvilinear Cubism

In the Boisgeloup studios in 1931 and 1932, Picasso, painting still lifes and portraits of Marie-Thérèse, developed a new style called Curvilinear Cubism. From 1923 on, Picasso's Cubist paintings had freer curved lines. The new still lifes and portraits had sweeping curves, circles, and contours, shapes he used to create earthy, sensual qualities. Picasso painted in brilliant colors and used black to outline the figures and shapes. In 1932 he did a long series of a seated or sleeping female figure. For example, in *The Dream* a woman sleeps in a chair with her hands folded in her lap. In *Girl Before a Mirror* a female figure on the left extends an arm and contemplates her own reflection on the right. The figures on both sides appear both clothed and nude at the same time. The double face on the left has an exposed profile painted plain, in cool lavender, plus a hidden front face painted in sun yellow and red. On the right Picasso enclosed the reflection in an oval and divided the two figures by a line. He also

The Dream, *with its sweeping curves and contours, is characteristic of Curvilinear Cubism.*

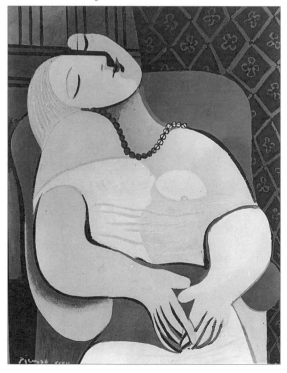

enclosed the reflected face within other ovals and distorted its features against a dark background.

Personal Dilemmas

Picasso's personal situation worsened in 1932, beginning four years of upheaval. First, Fernande Olivier published memoirs of her years with Picasso. While she presented an accurate picture of artists and Montmartre in the early 1900s, she presented Picasso as a physical and moral coward. Distressed by having this uncomplimentary version of his private life made public, Picasso tried to stop publication of the book but could not. In the spring of 1935 Picasso's marriage to Olga ended when she left with Paulo. The separation was bitter and the settlement fight worse. The official correspondence and hateful interviews with lawyers finally ended in a settlement that gave Olga a huge allowance, Château de Boisgeloup, and custody of Paulo; Picasso got the two-story flat in rue de la Boëtie and his art.

The indignity of the settlement fight with Olga upset Picasso so much that he could neither paint nor go to his upstairs studio. Late in 1935 he called Jaime Sabartés to come to Paris to help him and to work as a secretary. Sabartés and his wife came, helped Picasso get back to work, and stayed on for many years. In September 1935 the daughter of Picasso and Marie-Thérèse was born. They called her Maria de la Concepción, nicknamed Maya. Since the divorce from Olga was not yet final, Picasso could not marry Marie-Thérèse. He was troubled because he could not give the child a proper name,

Seated Bather

In Picasso: In the Collection of the Museum of Modern Art, *curator William Rubin describes the powerful effect created by* Seated Bather.

"In *Seated Bather* we are confronted by a hollowed-out creature whose hard, bonelike forms are at the opposite end of the spectrum from the early Cannes Bathers; they were all rubbery flesh, she all skeletal armor. While she sits in a comfortable pose against a deceptively placid [calm] sea and sky, the potential violence that Picasso finds in her . . . is epitomized by her mantislike head, which combines the themes of sexuality and aggression. The praying mantis, who devours her mate in the course of the sexual act, had been a favorite Surrealist symbol: as a number of Surrealist painters and poets collected mantises, they could hardly have escaped Picasso's notice."

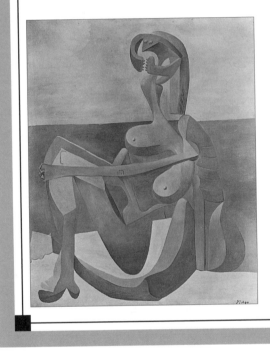

During Picasso's Bone Period, many of his paintings resembled sculptures made of bone. Oftentimes these paintings were disturbing, such as Seated Bather *(1929 or 1930). In this painting the woman's praying mantis head offers sharp contrast to her peaceful pose.*

but Picasso loved her, found comfort in her, and helped Marie-Thérèse take care of her.

During this turmoil, Picasso's inventive mind produced yet another kind of art, referred to as the Bone Period. Picasso painted figures that looked like sculptures made of bone. Many of them are ugly and disturbing. Perhaps most horrifying is *Seated Bather* (1929 or 1930). In this painting a female figure with a bone frame sits calmly on the sand by the sea and under a blue sky. The figure is painted in shades of white, and the colors of the sand, sea, and sky appear through her distorted frame. Her head is an insect, a praying mantis, with beady eyes and a vise-grip mouth.

Printmaking—A New Interest

During this decade Picasso developed his printmaking skills, teaching himself the tricks of engraving and etching. Afterward he made etchings to illustrate many books. In 1926 Picasso began a series of etchings to illustrate a new edition of *Le Chef-d'oeuvre Inconnu* (*The Unknown Masterpiece*), a book by Honoré de Balzac, in which a mad old painter spends ten years painting a woman, covering the picture over and over with scrawlings until it seems to him a masterpiece, while to others it is meaningless. For the book, Picasso engraved thirteen plates of the painter and his model, one of his favorite themes. *Painter with Model Knitting* (1927) most nearly illustrates the story. On the left a woman sits knitting; on the right a bald, bearded artist draws circles and scrawls on an easel placed between them.

In another print Picasso introduced the Minotaur, a new creature in his art, based on Greek mythology. On the island of Crete, King Minos had his craftsman Daedalus construct a labyrinth, a maze, to confine this monster, which was half-human, half-bull. Picasso made numerous ink drawings and etchings featuring the Minotaur. In *The Minotauromachy* (1935) Picasso combines the themes of the Minotaur and the bullfight. A little girl faces the beast with a candle and a bouquet. Between them a female torso lies across the back of a disemboweled horse. Nearby two young girls in a window gaze at doves, and a bearded man climbs a ladder to escape. Exquisitely drawn, it is nonetheless a strange scene, perhaps a part of Picasso's personal mythology.

Painter with Model Knitting *was engraved for Honoré de Balzac's* Le Chef-d'oeuvre Inconnu. *For this book, Picasso engraved a total of thirteen plates representing the theme of the painter and his model.*

In The Minotauromachy, *one of his many drawings and etchings featuring the Minotaur, Picasso incorporates both mythological and bullfighting themes.*

Success with the Public

A decade that had brought sadness and worry had also been rich in the creation of new techniques and new themes. It closed with an exhibition that increased Picasso's fame and popularity. Before 1932 artists admired him, but the public did not. For the retrospective exhibition in June and July 1932, Picasso selected two hundred pictures from all his periods, including the Blue, the Pink, the Negro, the Cubist, and the Bone, plus his latest canvases of Marie-Thérèse and some of the monsters. The opening brought together the wealthy and the elite of Paris. Biographer O'Brian says:

> He saw to the hanging of them [the pictures] himself; he set the sculptures in the proper light. He stated the case for his children [his works of art] to the best of his ability; he could do no more; and the verdict was to be given by others. . . .
>
> Picasso was there, neat and brushed, with his bow tie making one of its last appearances; he rarely attended his own shows, but this was no ordinary exhibition, and this time he received everybody who counted in the town. He had, as it were, put his cards on the table; and he won. The public, the social success was immense; the intellectual success greater still. . . . The retrospective . . . confirmed his reputation as one of the most important painters of the century, if not the most important.[48]

In 1936 another Picasso exhibition in Paris at the Gallerie Rosenberg was also a great success, but for this one Picasso went to Juan-les-Pins in the south of France to escape the limelight.

Chapter

6 War and *Guernica*, 1936–1945

After a brief unproductive period, Picasso took up his work again. Ambroise Vollard asked Picasso to make illustrations for a new edition of Georges-Louis Buffon's *Histoire naturelle*, an eighteenth-century book about animals. Over a two-year period Picasso made thirty-one aquatints of different animals. An aquatint is a process

Usually uninvolved in politics, Picasso worked for the cause of peace when civil war broke out in Spain in 1936.

of etching that can produce several tones, depending on how long a design is exposed to acid. To etch, an artist coats a copper plate with a layer of varnish, uses a sharp tool to carve a design into the varnish, and immerses the plate into an acid bath. The acid bites only into the areas where metal has been exposed by the carving. Then the plate can be inked for printing. Picasso took special care with these illustrations, presenting some animals in a lacy, decorative way and others, such as the ram, monumentally. All were realistically drawn.

Now single again, Picasso, with his new dog Elft and his friend Sabartés, took up socializing in cafés. Picasso met and greeted friends, Sabartés waited, and Elft went from table to table begging for sugar. In the cafés Picasso met Christian Zervos, editor of the art magazine *Les Cahiers d'Art*, and his wife Yvonne. And he met Surrealist poet Paul Éluard and his wife Nusch. Éluard, whose outlook on life resembled Picasso's, said that their views could "express the points that are common to all."[49] Paul Éluard introduced Picasso to Dora Maar, a professional photographer from Argentina. Strikingly attractive, with black hair, blue-green eyes, and high cheekbones, Maar was also an intellectual who spoke beautiful Spanish, qualities making

WAR AND *GUERNICA*, 1936–1945 ■ **63**

her attractive to Picasso. He painted his first portrait of her in November 1936.

Within the next year Picasso moved into two new studios. Since the Château de Boisgeloup now belonged to Olga, Vollard found Le Tremblay-sur-Mauldre, near Versailles, where Picasso converted a barn into a studio. In Paris, Picasso rented an old hotel at 7, rue des Grands-Augustins. Picasso used two upper floors for studios. Dora Maar, who had found the building for Picasso, lived around the corner. Though Picasso did not live with Dora Maar, she was his companion and friend for many years. Marie-Thérèse was also Picasso's companion during part of this time.

The Spanish Civil War

Picasso worried about Spain, where a civil war broke out in 1936 between the Spanish Fascists and the Spanish Republic. The Spanish Republic had been the constitutional government since its establishment in 1931. Because Spain did not prosper after the Republicans came to power, the Fascists, right-wing extremists led by Gen. Francisco Franco, were determined to overthrow the government.

Though Picasso usually stayed outside politics, in 1936 he felt he must become involved, since his own country was at war. Both he and Éluard denounced Fascist aggression and worked for the cause of peace. With his talent, fame, and money, Picasso supported the Republic. Spanish towns, including Málaga, were falling under Fascist control. Picasso set up feeding centers for children in Madrid and Barcelona and helped refugees, spending between three and four hundred thousand

francs in support of the Republic. (This was the equivalent of ten years' income for a Parisian earning a good living.) He sold paintings to help raise the money.

Germans and Italians, who had joined the Fascists, sent planes, guns, and tanks, and Germany sent bomber pilots. To raise more money, Picasso wrote and illustrated a comic book called *Sueño y Mentira de Franco (The Dream and Lie of Franco)*. He portrayed Franco as a horse and the Spanish people as a bull. In one frame the Franco monster attacks a beautiful classical head; in another it attacks the bull. As further support, Picasso promised the Spanish government that he would decorate a wall in the Spanish pavilion for the upcoming 1938 Paris World's Fair.

The events of April 26, 1937, gave Picasso his theme. Under Franco's orders, German planes attacked Guernica, a Basque town in northern Spain. The planes dropped bombs during the day, and soldiers shot inhabitants in the evening. Out of a population of 7,000, 1,654 died and 889 were wounded. The world was stunned. Picasso was angry and indignant. On May 1 Picasso made sketches of a dying horse, a bull, and a woman holding a lamp. From May 1 until mid-June, he worked feverishly on a picture he called *Guernica*. He wanted this painting to be an indictment, or accusation, of evil, an expression of his loathing for "the military caste that has plunged Spain into a sea of suffering and death."[50]

Guernica

Picasso made over fifty studies for the picture. By May 11 he had the composition outlined on a canvas measuring 25 feet 5 inches by 11 feet 5 inches. Picasso's companion Dora Maar photographed the picture at seven different stages while Picasso painted it. *Guernica* is a Cubist work done with planes and distortion, painted entirely in black, gray, and white. Its symbolic figures portray the emotional terror and suffering caused by war.

In the upper center of the picture, a woman stretches from an open window. Her long arm holds an oil lamp lighting the front part of a shrieking horse with a lance pierced through its back. Under the horse's hooves a man's shattered body lies with one hand outstretched above his head and the other clutching a broken sword beside a flower. The triangle of light also illuminates a partly clothed woman facing upward with a dazed stare. On bare, fat feet, she flees, labored and crouching, her knee bloated into a triangle. On the left, a black bull, with body in shadow and white head in light, has an indifferent, humanlike face. At the edges two women shriek their frozen cries, faces turned upward. The mother on the left holds her dead child. The woman on the right stands before her burning house. Over the scene an electric lightbulb glows within a shade and emits short jagged rays, at once signifying the sun dimmed and the eye watching. Behind all, in the dark shadows a bird screeches on its perch.

In support of the Spanish Republic during the Spanish Civil War, Picasso wrote and illustrated a comic book, The Dream and Lie of Franco.

A crying woman from a study for Guernica *conveys the terror and suffering caused by war.*

To read the painting, the eye moves through a series of triangular and oval planes, trapezoids, and rectangles. The dead man's hands and the fleeing woman's feet form the base of a large triangle, its sides made by the edge of the lamp's glow and the bird's perch. Its apex, or tip, is unclear; both the oil lamp and the electric light stand near, but neither at the apex. Smaller triangles make up the heads of the women. Triangles help shape the dying horse's body and form tongues, fingers, flames, the bull's ears, and the dead child's inverted nose. Gouged-out ovals form suffering heads. And the same flattened oval that forms the lightbulb's shade recurs in the bull's eyes and in the eyes of the suffering and dying. Trapezoids and rectangles make structures for body parts, windows, a door, boards, and the bull's backdrop. The bull's white tail rises like a natural flame on the left, balancing the artificial flames of the fire that set the woman's dwelling ablaze on the right.

Reactions to *Guernica*

From the moment of the pavilion's opening, *Guernica* caused excitement, admiration, and controversy as a propaganda piece. Viewers who supported the civil war criticized it; those who opposed the Fascists praised it. Its symbols make an allegory, a symbolic statement condemning war's brutality, the evil and stupidity of brute power, and the terrible suffering of innocent people. Picasso said, "The bull there represents brutality, the horse the people. Yes, there I used symbolism."[51] The painting also asserts that no one wins. There is no victory, for the bull stands in a desolate battlefield where all decency, art, and humanity have vanished.

At first, viewers saw *Guernica* as a commentary only on a past event, but as World War II unfolded, they saw it as a prophecy. Biographer Pierre Daix explains:

We are obsessed, assaulted by the implacable [unforgiving] architecture of the picture. This is no historical painting to divert the spectator. Nothing separates us from the women screaming in terror as death falls senselessly from the sky. We find ourselves caught between the noble horse struck down and the bull, a brutal force of darkness. We are not just being told a story. No divine power is there to relieve us. The calamity is ours, experienced under a sun made by human hands. *Guer-*

Highly controversial and highly praised, Guernica *is an indictment of the evils of war and the emotional suffering incurred by innocent people. Painted in true Cubist form,* Guernica *is composed of numerous planes and distorted perspectives.*

nica is the first historical picture painted for men consciously in the act of making their own history. It is the mirror-image of a world of atrocity and bestiality from which it is man's duty to emerge.[52]

Picasso saw the Spanish Fascists fighting against people, against freedom. Like the people in this fight, Picasso felt he had spent his whole life bombarded with pressures to conform to artistic tradition, a denial of his freedom as an artist.

The Spanish Civil War continued as more and more small towns fell into Fascist hands. By the end of 1938 the Republic had lost. Barcelona fell in January 1939, and Madrid in March, ending the struggle. During this same period, Picasso's mother died in Barcelona, and in July his friend Ambroise Vollard died. It was a sad year for Picasso. In the fall of

1939 he left for Royan, a village near Bordeaux on the west coast of France, where he stayed until 1941, except for short trips to Paris.

Picasso intended to give *Guernica* to Spain when the Republic had been restored. After the Paris World's Fair the Museum of Modern Art in New York kept the painting until it was moved to Madrid in the late 1980s. There it hangs in the Reina Sofia Museum, an old hospital converted into a museum of modern art. The painting hangs in its own alcove adjacent to a main room of the museum. A clear plastic shield separates the public from the painting. Apparently the civil war's emotions still linger in Spain, strong enough that curators take no risk that the painting will trigger a violent reaction in someone who would want to vandalize it.

In the main room hang some forty sketches Picasso made in preparation for

Guernica, as well as several of his post-scripts. Among them are six women's faces, sad and desperate. The distortion and ugliness of the faces depict the anguish the women must have felt from cruelty imposed on them and their powerlessness to stop it. In one, a woman with a green face tears frantically at a blue handkerchief.

Other Wartime Paintings

While working on pictures related to the war, Picasso painted portraits of people close to him. Two paintings—*Portrait of Dora Maar* (1937) and *Portrait of Marie-Thérèse* (1937)—contrast the differences between the two women's personalities. Picasso painted Dora Maar as a beautiful, sophisticated woman, dressed elegantly in a black top decorated with bright embroidery. He painted Marie-Thérèse as a fair-haired, serene woman in a pastel-colored sweater and a hat with a curved brim. Both sit in chairs: Dora in one with straight lines and angles, Marie-Thérèse in one with curves. Dora's arms and hands have angles, and her fingernails are red and pointed. Marie-Thérèse's arms and hands have curves and short, yellow fingernails. Both faces have frontal and profile views. By skillfully juxtaposing, or

The differences in the portraits of Dora Maar (left) and Marie-Thérèse (right) reflect their individual personalities. Dora is elegant and sophisticated; Marie-Thérèse is feminine and youthful.

placing together, mauve, yellow, green, and pink pigments, Picasso gave Dora's complexion a luminous quality. The highlighted white shading into blue and the yellow of her lips suggest Marie-Thérèse's easygoing nature. The white space surrounding Dora, painted with enclosing lines, seems too weak to confine her spirited nature. In a room with a dark floor and gray walls rising to a white ceiling, Marie-Thérèse appears as if she could float in and out freely. Besides depicting the women's personalities, the portraits suggest the nature of Picasso's relationships with them.

In three other portraits of people close to him, Picasso presents each with appreciation. In *Portrait of Nusch Éluard* (1937) the elegance of the woman's coat

In Maya with a Doll, *Picasso portrays his daughter (by Marie-Thérèse) in a colorful pinafore. Her highlighted face is distorted, showing both frontal and profile views.*

enhances the beauty of her face. Curator Hélène Seckel writes "The face, which is divided between night and day, yellow and blue, sunlight and moonshine, shown in both frontal and profile views . . . reveals the young woman's sensitivity."[53] *Maya with a Doll* (1938) shows the lively daughter of Marie-Thérèse and Picasso wearing a bright, embroidered pinafore. As in the painting of her mother, Maya has fair hair and a highlighted face. Distorted for both frontal and profile views, her face contrasts with the doll's face, which has nose and eyes in realistic places. In *Jaime Sabartés* (1939) Picasso painted his friend wearing the ruff and black plumed hat of a Spanish gentleman. The midsection of his face puts his left cheek where his nose would be and his nose where his right cheek would be. Upside down, his glasses frame eyes made as crosses. Though distorted, Picasso's presentation of his friend is done with elegant good humor.

The Beginning of World War II

While in Royan, Picasso followed the news about Hitler's army as it advanced in the spring of 1940 through Holland and Belgium and drove the French army south. By June Germans had come to Paris—and to Royan—put France under German occupation, and hunted openly for Jews. Suspected of being part Jewish, Picasso was frightened for his safety, but more frightened that his pictures, scattered in studios around Paris, might be destroyed in German bombing raids. He left Royan for Paris, ordered dozens of crates, and started to pack. But the works were too

How Sabartés's Portrait Came About

In A Picasso Anthology: Documents, Criticism, Reminiscences, *Marilyn McCully quotes Jaime Sabartés's explanation of how his portrait came about.*

"It was my idea. It was a whim. I had always dreamed of being painted by Picasso as a sixteenth-century nobleman. . . . And when you mention that sort of whim to Picasso, it's not as if you were talking to a deaf man. . . . He made some sketches first—in 1938, at the rue La Boëtie—and that collar with the starched ruff amused him. He was planning to paint a full-length, life-size portrait in this costume of a grandee [noble] of Spain. . . . I thought he had forgotten about it, though, and then one day in Royan he surprised me with this. Did you notice that he used the colourings of the Spanish paintings of that period?"

Jaime Sabartés, *shown with a distorted face, wears the attire of a Spanish gentleman.*

scattered—there were too many—and he gave up in discouragement, knowing that his special pieces were already stored in a safe-deposit vault in a bank.

In 1941 during German occupation Picasso went back to Paris and stayed there for the duration of the war. Friends urged him to escape to America or to a place that offered him safety. But he refused, believing that to do anything but go on with his art would acknowledge victory for the Germans. In July and August of 1942 the police swept through Paris and rounded up Jews, resisters, communists, and other suspected people, deporting trainloads of them through France to concentration camps in Auschwitz, Dachau, and Buchenwald. Nazis shot two hundred hostages

Picasso leans from the window of his studio in Paris. Although Picasso's art was considered "degenerate" by the Nazis, neither Picasso nor his art was harmed during the German occupation.

outside Paris in August and September of that year, and people lived in fear that the Gestapo would come for them during the night. Germans confiscated property of Jews and Gentiles alike.

When German police inspected the bank vaults that held Picasso's and Matisse's works, Picasso led them in and out of the rooms so fast and talked about so many strange-looking paintings that the police became confused and left, thinking they had inspected them all. The police routinely went to Picasso's studios, but they could find nothing suspicious in the messy rooms. Picasso never tried to bargain or to argue; according to biographer O'Brian, he only smiled, gave them postcards of *Guernica*, and said, "Souvenir, sou-

venir." One German officer asked him, "Did you do this?" and Picasso replied, "No, you did," but the officer did not understand. The Nazis hated Picasso's art, called it "degenerate," and might have burned it, but for some mysterious reason, never did, nor ever took Picasso prisoner. Though Picasso was just as afraid as others, his presence in Paris and his determination to paint there gave comfort to his friends and even to those who had only heard about him.

Life in Occupied Paris

During the years of occupation Picasso felt bored and confined; it was one of the

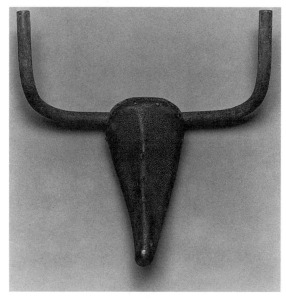

From his junk collection, Picasso created Head of a Bull *using a bicycle seat and handlebars.*

loneliest periods of his life, he said. Picasso visited Marie-Thérèse and Maya every Thursday and Sunday. But much of the time he stayed at home with Dora and Kazbec, their new Afghan hound. Since the Germans confiscated coal to send to

Germany, there was little fuel. No taxis operated and few buses or trains ran, and there was no gasoline for cars. The electricity was often shut off, the studios went unheated, and art supplies were scarce. Picasso's painting reflected "a somber, agonizing cruelty which suggests better than any description could do, the intolerable atmosphere of those days," according to Elgar and Maillard.[54]

Picasso set up a sculpture studio in the bathroom, the smallest and warmest room in the house. In his collection of junk, he found an old leather bicycle seat and a rusty pair of handlebars. "In a flash, they became associated in my mind," Picasso recalled, and he made *Head of a Bull* (1942) and cast it in bronze. Picasso said, "One should be able to take a bit of wood and find [that] it's a bird."[55] In other words, the art is in the creating, not the materials. Picasso also did a bronze piece, *Death's Head* (1943), described by Hélène Seckel:

This frightening visage of death seems to have come . . . out of the depths of

Wartime Paris

In Picasso, *Biographer Patrick O'Brian describes Paris under German occupation.*

"The Paris to which [Picasso] returned was a strange, dark city, its lights reduced to a sinister pale-blue glow: the curfew, rationing, endless queues [lines] for food and for permits of every kind. And although at first it was sparsely inhabited by Parisians, since the Germans had taken huge numbers of prisoners and multitudes had fled, the streets were filled with hateful uniforms, gray, green, and black; and the swastika flew over countless buildings, while the Louvre stood dark and empty."

time, or some bone-heap left by the war still raging all around. To be sure, this motif . . . was related to contemporary events, but it also has a more universal meaning and belongs to the long line of meditations on this theme in Western . . . sculpture. The few details—eyesockets, nose cavity, barely visible clenched teeth—suffice to give it an amazingly realistic presence. The polished bronze makes it look like a stone eroded through the ages, gradually losing all trace of humanity.[56]

In February 1943 Picasso sculpted a large statue of a bearded shepherd carrying a frightened lamb, *Man with a Sheep*. The shepherd's hands are out of proportion, his legs and flat feet are barely modeled, and he holds the sheep out of balance for the way he stands. This large figure belongs to the classical tradition in sculpture, but Picasso made his own variations. Critics have tried to make the shepherd a Christian symbol of the Good Shepherd, but Picasso insisted he had no symbolic intent. Seckel quotes him: "The man could just as well be carrying a pig instead of a sheep. There is nothing symbolic about it. It is beautiful, that's all."[57]

Painting Through the War

Late in 1941 the United States entered World War II, turning it in the Allies' favor. In June 1944 the Allies landed in France on the English Channel coast, and the Germans had to retreat, becoming more violent as they tried to destroy Paris before they lost it. Outside of Paris they massacred everyone in sight, burning 634

Although Man with a Sheep *was sculpted in the classical tradition, Picasso varied proportions to create a unique work.*

men, women, and children in a village church. During the violence and chaos Picasso went right on painting. Once a bullet came through his window, missing him by an inch as he painted. In mid-August Picasso went to stay with Marie-Thérèse and Maya until the liberation of Paris two weeks later. Biographer Patrick O'Brian describes the situation:

With the strange, unorganized battle going on all around him, and with the likelihood of a German tank in any street or a *milicien* [soldier] with a rifle on any rooftop, killing for the sake of killing now that all hope was gone, he [Picasso] made his way to Marie-Thérèse's flat on the Ile Saint-Louis, the best part of a mile away, where there was very heavy fighting. Here he painted two careful portraits of his daughter, a sweet child now, . . . and the head of a young woman.[58]

The War Ends

On August 25, 1944, the Allies liberated Paris, and World War II ended in the summer of 1945. Following the liberation, poets, painters, art critics, museum directors, and writers, all wearing Allied uniforms, invaded Picasso's studio to salute him as a symbol of freedom. Officers and ordinary soldiers thronged up the stairway to his studios in a mass, and Picasso greeted them all.

7 Fame and Wealth, 1945–1954

When the war ended, both Picasso and the city of Paris came back to life. During his stay with Marie-Thérèse and Maya in the last weeks of the war, Picasso's absence from his own quarters started a rumor that the Germans had taken him hostage when they retreated. After a short time, however, he returned to rue des Grands-Augustins, and the "whole world rang with the news," according to Patrick O'Brian.[59] The publicity was only the beginning of the attention Picasso was to receive in the next years.

Realizing that fighting against oppression with his art alone was no longer enough, Picasso had joined the French Communist Party in October 1944. He viewed the French Communists as an organization working to promote world understanding and freedom for people. As a person who had felt like an outsider all his life, Picasso welcomed the warm acceptance given him by the French Communists. His name, of course, brought publicity to the party, and Picasso received many invitations to attend conferences. His first was the Congress of Intellectuals for Peace in Warsaw, Poland, in 1948, when he traveled for the first time by airplane.

The end of the war also brought renewed interest in art, particularly in Picasso's. In the years between 1944 and 1954, at least nineteen exhibitions showed Picasso's works. Many of them were major shows in large cities outside of Paris—London; Lyons, France; Rome and Milan, Italy; São Paulo, Brazil; and New York. The same period saw at least five books published about Picasso and his art, plus a documentary film. Good color photographs reproduced his paintings for exhibition catalogs, making his work accessible to an even wider audience.

Indifferent to Wealth

As Picasso's reputation grew, so too did the number of visitors and his wealth. Famous people, like French writers Jean-Paul Sartre and André Malraux, came to see him. His paintings had begun to sell for enormous sums of money. Money had once symbolized success and flattered him, but he grew indifferent to its worth. He never bothered to invest, and after his death, his heirs found a forgotten box of gold coins and, stuffed in drawers and cupboards, bundles of banknotes, some no longer current.

By the end of the war Picasso's relationship with Dora Maar had become strained. By chance in a café in 1943,

Picasso and his friends met two young women who claimed to be painters. Picasso casually invited them to his studio. Both came once, but one of them, Françoise Gilot, came again and again. Twenty-two years old at the time she met Picasso, Gilot had given up the study of law to become a painter. She had red hair, a fine oval face, intelligence and charm. Though Picasso was indifferent to her at first, in 1946 her face began to appear in his pictures.

Lithography

In 1946 Picasso was sixty-five years old, the age most people retire, but few have the creative power and energy Picasso had at that age. His annual output staggered younger men. He had discovered Fernand Mourlot's lithography studio in November 1945, where he often worked ten and eleven hours a day. He made more than two hundred lithographs over the next

Mastering lithography, Picasso produced a series of lithographs featuring Françoise Gilot. A 1946 lithograph of Gilot is shown here.

Picasso's Response to Fame

Picasso was uncomfortable with fame. In Picasso, *biographer Pierre Daiz gives his interpretation of Picasso's discomfort.*

"There is some reflex in his blood, a reflex which is not so much Mediterranean as characteristic of those stony countries where the gods live at the level of the clouds, and where men instinctively draw back from anything that goes beyond reasonable bounds. . . . As far as Picasso is concerned, he was born with a faculty of self-criticism, not only in his art, but in every one of his gestures, all his reactions."

three and a half years. To make a lithograph, an artist draws on a stone or on a sheet of zinc or aluminum with oily ink. The undrawn parts are treated and made wet to repel the oily substance. When the artist prints, the lines and spaces covered with oily ink make the design. As usual, Picasso mastered the technique quickly, made tools for himself, and invented new techniques.

He used lithography for many themes. For example, Picasso did a series of lithographs after *David and Bathsheba*, a 1526 painting by German painter Lucas Cranach the Elder. Like Cranach's painting, Picasso's interpretations, called *David and Bathsheba, After Cranach the Elder* (1947 and 1949), portrays the biblical King David on a balcony, watching the beautiful Bathsheba being bathed. Picasso made two lithographs, one positive (black lines on white background) and one negative (white lines on black background). Picasso also did a series of animals; for example, he printed eleven progressive lithographs titled *Bull*, from December 1945 to January 1946.

In this same year Françoise Gilot appeared for the first time in Picasso's art. In May he painted her on a large canvas, as a flower—*Woman Flower*—with a long blue stem for a body, long pods for arms, round pieces of fruit for her breasts, a side oval for her face, and dark green leaves for her hair. With a few simple lines he painted her face, but the features are unmistakably those of Françoise. In addition, Picasso did a series of lithographs of her head.

A Château in Antibes

Starting in 1946, Picasso spent more time in the south of France near the Italian border. Several villages and towns along the Mediterranean coastline lie close to one another, with mountains rising just beyond them: Nice, Antibes, Golfe-Juan, Juan-Les-Pins, Cannes, and farther up from the sea, Vallauris and Mougins. During the summer in Golfe-Juan with Françoise, he met Dor de la Souchère, who offered Picasso a chance to paint in a

Joie de Vivre *depicts Françoise Gilot as a dancing flower surrounded by centaurs and fauns.*

room on the upper floors of the Château d'Antibes. Antibes is an old city, once an ancient Greek city called Antipolis. From 1385 to 1608, a ruling Italian family named Grimaldi inhabited the château, an imposing square building with a tower, built on a rock high above the sea. In 1927 the town of Antibes purchased the crumbling château to install a museum.

Picasso worked in the Château d'Antibes, also called Musée Grimaldi, from July to December. When he had finished, he left behind 175 works: paintings, ceramics, drawings, lithographs, a tapestry, and two sculptures. Because he felt these works are suited to a certain light, atmosphere, and space, Picasso requested that none of them ever leave the original setting. According to de la Souchère, Picasso repeated many times, "If you want to see the Picasso of Antibes, you must come to Antibes."[60] Sometime in the following decade the museum was renamed from Musée Grimaldi to Musée Picasso.

In the château Picasso painted mythological centaurs and fauns. A centaur is half-horse and half-man. A faun as it is called in Roman mythology, is the same as the satyr in Greek mythology, part goat, part man, who lived in wild places—thickets, forests, and mountains. God of goatherds and shepherds, the Greek god Pan was part human and part animal with goat horns and goat hoofs. A wonderful musician, he played on his reed pipes and made melodies as sweet as a nightingale's song. He danced with woodland nymphs and fell in love with one nymph after another, but they rejected him because he was ugly. Late in 1946 Françoise became the nymph in a long series of pencil drawings telling the story of Pan, his song, dance, and rejection.

The major work in the museum is *Joie de Vivre*, the same title Matisse used for a painting. In a style that hints of Matisse's work, Picasso painted Françoise in the center as a flower dancing. Around her centaurs and fauns play simple musical instruments. The figures, painted in pale blue, white, and deep red, dance and play on yellow sand against a blue sky and deep-blue sea on which a boat with a yellow sail moves. A happy, romantic form, this pastoral, or rural scene, fuses human and animal, or natural, worlds. In these pieces Picasso attains the calm and clarity of Greek art, but he used his own means of expressing, as Pierre Daix says, "renewed happiness, his materialistic confidence in life, the harmony of nature, peace regained. It is a song of victory over the night."[61]

Becoming a Potter

After a productive and happy year Picasso and Françoise went back to Paris for the winter. In May 1947 Picasso and Françoise's son Claude was born. Shortly after, the three of them went to Vallauris. A village just up the hill from Golfe-Juan, Vallauris has produced pottery for thousands of years because the nearby clay is especially suitable. A year earlier Picasso had met Georges and Suzanne Ramié, who owned a pottery factory; under their guidance Picasso had tried a few pieces. In the summer of 1947 he bought a house in the village and settled down for serious study. He loved the feel of clay and the atmosphere of Vallauris with its artisans and peasants.

Picasso stayed a year, learning to work the wheels, the kilns, and the clays. He made two thousand pieces in one year. His goal was the act of creating. "I have less and less time, and yet I have more and more to say," he said, as quoted by Jean

Sutherland Boggs.[62] He made pots, plates, and figures of animals. He glazed them with images of bulls, the sun, animals, birds, fish, and women's bodies. For him ceramics fused three-dimensional form with the language of color. Moreover, Picasso felt that this art entered people's lives; common people could have beautiful things to use.

Before Picasso worked in Vallauris, the pottery industry had been dying out. Today pottery shops line the long street leading up the hill. Behind the shops are small factories where artisans make fine wares. The factory where Picasso learned this art

During his stay in Vallauris, Picasso helped the pottery industry to prosper. Picasso's Third Vallauris Poster, *created in 1948, advertises an exposition of pottery, flowers, and perfume.*

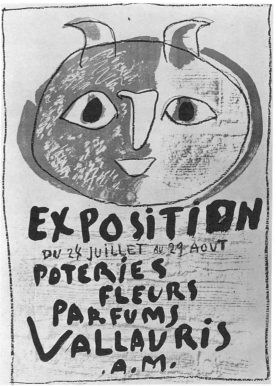

is now a museum displaying the wheels and kilns he used. A wax likeness of Picasso shows him at a wheel attending to his work in fixed concentration, and a live working potter demonstrates how to throw a pot. Farther up the hill another museum displays rooms full of Picasso's ceramics. The smooth jugs and pitchers have graceful lines, and the faces on plates express humor and whimsy. They are beautiful pieces.

Back in Paris Picasso was asked to prepare a poster for a peace conference to be held there in 1949. Picasso made a lithograph of a white pigeon on a black background, a symbolic dove of peace. The poster, which became one of Picasso's most popular works, appeared around the world. In April Picasso and Françoise's daughter was born. They named her

In a return to the themes of mother and child, Picasso depicted his family in Maternity with Orange.

Paloma, the Spanish word for *dove* after the dove of peace shown on posters all around Paris. Claude and Paloma brought Picasso's attention back to the themes of mother and child and of children playing. For example, he painted *Claude and Paloma*, in 1950, and *Maternity with Orange*, in 1951.

Honors and a Temple in Vallauris

After five years of peace following World War II, the Korean War broke out in the summer of 1950. Disturbed by the outbreak of another war, Picasso went to Vallauris. There the citizens, expressing their appreciation to him for his revitalizing their village, made him an honorary citizen. In turn Picasso expressed his appreciation by giving Vallauris one of the three bronze statues of *Man with a Sheep* to place in the main square near the ceramics museum. In 1951 Vallauris celebrated Picasso's seventieth birthday with a great feast and gave him a fourteenth-century chapel next to the ceramics museum. It was a small chapel with a beautiful vaulted ceiling.

Picasso turned the chapel into a temple of peace. Working on plywood panels that would be installed in the chapel later, he painted *War* on one panel and *Peace* on another. In *War* Picasso painted a black cloud and a fiery red background where shadowy soldiers hold guns. In the foreground Picasso used classical symbols: the god of war, swords, shields, and Perseus, who slew the snake-haired Medusa. On the *Peace* panel, in the tradition of folktales and fairy tales, he depicted whole-

The Dove Rises

In Life with Picasso, *Françoise Gilot and Carlton Lake explain how the peace dove poster came into being.*

"In his aviary, in company with many exotic birds, Matisse had four large Milanese pigeons. Their feet were not bare like most pigeons. They had feathers right down to the ground covering their claws; it was just as though the feet had white gaiters on them. One day he said to Pablo, 'I ought to give these to you because they look like some you've already painted.' We took them back to Vallauris with us. One of them had a very distinguished artistic and political career. Early in 1949 Pablo made a lithograph of it which turned out to be a brilliant technical success. . . .

About a month later, the poet and novelist Louis Aragon, who served as a kind of intellectual wheelhorse for the French Communist Party, came to the studio in the Rue des Grands-Augustins to prod Pablo into giving him a sketch he had promised him for the poster. . . . Aragon looked through a folder of recent lithographs, and when he saw that one, the pigeon looked so much like a dove to him that he had the idea of making it the symbol of the [peace] congress. Pablo agreed and by the end of the day, the poster and the 'dove' had already begun to appear on Paris walls."

DEUXIÈME
CONGRÈS MONDIAL
DES PARTISANS
DE LA PAIX
LONDRES
13·19 NOVEMBRE 1950

Symbolizing peace, Picasso's dove graced the poster for the Second World Conference of the Partisans of Peace.

some work and imaginative fun. Figures prepare fire, tend the young, and draw. A child plows the earth with a tame Pegasus, the great flying horse of Greek mythology. A faun pipes, a blindfolded woman juggles, one child fishes for birds, and another floats and balances a cage of fish. Over all, a bright sun bursts into leaves. On a third panel Picasso painted a dove of peace rising. This panel ties the other two together thematically. Picasso completed the panels in 1952, and they were installed in 1954. Art critic Michel Leiris spoke of the chapel as a balance between hope and fear, a message that expresses a longing for peace and goodwill.

Junk Sculpture

In 1948 Picasso bought an abandoned perfume factory to use as a place to store

Girl Jumping Rope *was constructed from junk collected at the Vallauris dump.*

his ceramics and to work on sculptures. He constructed entire statues from junk collected at the Vallauris town dump by pressing pieces directly into plaster. He made *The She Goat* (1950) using a cropped palm frond for the goat's back, an old wicker basket for her pregnant belly, pieces of knotted wood and metal for her legs, a twisted piece of metal for her tail, grapevine roots for her beard and horns, a tin can for her sternum, and two earthenware pots for her udders. Picasso then cast the assembled parts in bronze. Still a delight for viewers, the original, uncast assemblage stands on display in the Musée Picasso in Paris. He also made *Baboon and Young* (1951) using two of Claude's toy cars for the head and junk for the rest.

Another junk sculpture fulfilled one of Picasso's dreams—to make a weightless piece that did not touch the ground, a seeming impossibility for a standing sculpture. With *Girl Jumping Rope* (1950) Picasso caught the girl jumping up as the rope touched the ground. A rope of bent metal holds up the entire statue. The girl has a chocolate-box face and corrugated-cardboard hair. Her body is a wicker basket, and her skirt newspaper. At the end of her short wooden legs, she wears oversized, unmatched shoes. Hélène Seckel says, "This touching and humorous figure is a perfect image of childhood: a well-groomed little girl, who looks very proper, blithely skipping rope, her skirts flying; in play, she has put on shoes that are too big for her feet."[63]

Sadness Again

Beginning early in 1952 Picasso went through another depressing period. His

Although pictured happily together in 1951 at the celebration of Picasso's seventieth birthday, Françoise Gilot and Pablo Picasso's relationship was faltering. In 1953 the couple separated.

relationship with Françoise was deteriorating and in the summer of 1953 she took the children and left him. His good friend Paul Éluard died suddenly late in 1952 at a time when Matisse was very ill. Trying to drive out his misery, Picasso took up a frenzied social life, traveling to bars, celebrations, and bullfights. He invited Eduoard Pignon, a young, unknown painter friend, and his wife Hélène Parmelin Pignon, a writer, to live and work in the upper floor of the perfume factory. The partnership worked well. The two artists shared work with one another, and Picasso was less lonely. In 1954 Picasso's friend Matisse died. Picasso was too deeply affected to talk; he said, "Since Matisse is gone, there is nothing whatsoever to be said."[64]

As had happened in previous periods of discontent, Picasso expressed his state of mind in his art. Between late 1952 and early 1954, Picasso did 180 drawings of the artist and model, his second series on this theme. When the series was published in the magazine *Verve*, Michel Leiris's preface called it "a visual journal of a detestable season in hell, a crisis of his inner life which led him on to the widest kind of questioning."[65] This series portrays old, doddering painters, a romantic young man, women painters, even a monkey. There are perplexed, beautiful, and abstract models. As Leiris said, Picasso had thrown his whole life onto the scales to "wrench from his art the very meaning of life."[66] Then he stopped making the drawings. At the end of 1954 Picasso went on to paint *Portrait of Mm. Z*, the subject of which was about to enter his life in a permanent way.

8 A Bountiful Old Age, 1954–1973

During the frenzied summer of 1953, Picasso made several trips to Perpignan, a French town near the Spanish border, as the guest of his friend Jacques dé Lazerme and his wife. While there he met divorcée Jacqueline Roque, who followed Picasso to Vallauris and helped in a pottery factory during the winter. When Picasso again visited the Lazermes in the summer of 1954, Jacqueline unexpectedly joined them. Picasso treated her disagreeably; she treated him with submission and devotion. Finally they worked out their differences and returned to Vallauris.

Early in 1955, Picasso's former wife Olga died of cancer in a hospital in Cannes. Picasso and she had never completely cut off their relationship; he kept her photograph on display and had worn her ring since their wedding. When she died, Picasso buried her. By spring 1955 Picasso and Françoise were fighting over the house in Vallauris, and Françoise got ownership. Consequently, Picasso, who had liked the house and hated change, had to find a new home. During the summer he bought La Californie in Cannes, a large house with a view of Golfe-Juan and the sea. He moved there with Jacqueline, her daughter Kathy, his dogs, and a pet goat.

Forced out of his home in Vallauris upon his separation, Picasso purchased La Californie in Cannes. This beautiful home overlooked Golfe-Juan and the sea.

A Movie and Growing Fame

During the summer of 1955, when Picasso was seventy-five, Henri-Georges Clouzot directed a full-length color film about Picasso—*Le Mystère Picasso.* Shot in the hot sun on the beach near Antibes, the film shows how Picasso composed his work and the way he made changes as he painted. He worked at his easel and got up every few seconds to let the camerapeople film his last brush strokes. Working sometimes twelve hours a day, he painted bullfights, still lifes, and nudes, and made collages for the film. Biographer Patrick O'Brian describes the scene:

> The most astonishing thing about the whole undertaking was the way he carried on his solitary pursuit amid a host of directors, cameramen, technicians, and idle spectators, perpetually interrupted yet never for a moment losing his concentration, sitting there with his brown [tanned] person shining with sweat, clothed in a pair of canvas drawers [shorts], his luminous eye fixed upon his picture and his hand sweeping out the perfect curves.[67]

Although the project took tremendous energy, Picasso enjoyed the filming techniques and liked the crew.

Worldwide Exhibitions

By the late 1950s, Picasso's fame had spread, and many cities held well-attended exhibitions. In 1955 in Paris his paintings were shown in one exhibition and his drawings in another. New York's Museum of Modern Art held a second retrospective in 1957. Other exhibitions were held in Brussels, Belgium; Amsterdam, Holland; Cologne and Hamburg, Germany; and Tokyo, Japan. He lent one hundred pictures from his own collection for the exhibition at the prestigious Tate Gallery in London, a show attended by 450,000 people. Photographer and friend Brassaï asked Picasso why he never went to the exhibitions. Picasso explained:

> Why should I waste my time going to see my paintings again? I have a good memory, and I remember all of them. I loaned a great many of my canvases to the exhibition [at the Tate Gallery], and that gave me quite enough trouble. . . . Exhibitions don't mean a great deal to me anymore. My old paintings no longer interest me. I'm much more curious about those I haven't yet done.[68]

At seventy-five Picasso had many works to come. In 1956 Norwegian painter and sculptor Carl Nesjar introduced him to a technique for using sandblasted concrete, allowing him to produce sculptures on an architectural scale. Over the years he made about a dozen huge figures in concrete mixed with gravel, cut out with electric chisels. *Woman with Outstretched Arms* (1961) began as a sheet of paper torn from a spiral notebook, folded into a woman whose right-hand fingers were fringes from the torn sheet. From the paper model Picasso made a seven-foot wire-mesh and sheetmetal model and painted it white. In 1962 Carl Nesjar placed a concrete version of the statue, called *The Angel,* on the grounds of art dealer Daniel-Henry Kahnweiler's home. Picasso also designed huge sculptures of concrete, bent sheet iron, and metal cutouts for Oslo, Norway; Barcelona, Spain; Marseilles, France; Stockholm, Sweden; and Chicago, Illinois.

The villa La Californie, with its hillside view of the sea and its lush surrounding gardens, became the subject of many paintings. Picasso painted landscapes from different windows in the house—*The*

The Chicago Picasso

In A Picasso Anthology, *Marilyn McCully quotes an excerpt from Roland Penrose's* Scrap Book. *A friend of Picasso, Penrose explains how he helped architects engage Picasso to make a sculpture for the Chicago Civic Center.*

"The architects wanted an introduction to Picasso so that they could persuade him to design a maquette [a model of an intended work] which could be enlarged to gigantic proportions. . . . I knew well enough how obstinate Don Pablo could be and how he systematically turned down any proposals that meant accepting a commission. In this case, however, realizing the importance of the project, I reluctantly accepted the difficult task of helping the Chicago architects to gain Picasso's interest. . . .

In spite of [his current projects], Picasso began to warm to the idea. . . .

In fact it was nearly a year later that suddenly I found two versions of a large head made of sheet iron and rods, unlike anything I had seen around before. . . .

Another year passed and the head remained untouched . . . , but when I arranged another visit . . . serious progress in the complicated transformations of the head from maquette to monument began. The maquette

then left for Chicago and was placed in the hands of skilled engineers. In the summer of 1967 the great sculpture in cor-ten steel was unveiled by the Mayor of Chicago. . . . From the start [Picasso] had refused to discuss payment in any form but [the architects' representative] . . . brought with him a cheque for $100,000 which he presented to Picasso as a token of their gratitude. This Don Pablo refused categorically saying he wished the sculpture to be a gift to the people of Chicago. It will in this way remain dominating the great central plaza, a unique monument to his genius and his generosity."

Picasso's maquette for the Chicago Civic Center.

The surroundings of La Californie were captured in many of Picasso's paintings, such as The Bay at Cannes *in which the rooftops and sea curve together.*

Bay at Cannes (1958) and *The Hillside at La Californie* (1959). The Cannes paintings have brilliant roofs and sea colors, curves, and varied composition. Picasso also painted interior landscapes, scenes of his studio in different lights with different objects. For example, in *The Pigeons* (1957) Picasso painted white pigeons against a frame that reflects yellow and orange light. The frame encloses a view of the sea, palms, and rooftops.

Art Inspired by a Past Artist

Although Picasso had painted his own versions of other artists' works throughout his life, in his older years he took inspiration from other artists more frequently. In 1957 he began transforming Spanish painter Diego Velázquez's *Las Meninas* (*The Maids of Honor*) (1656) into a series of forty-four paintings. In the Velázquez painting an artist stands at work at the side of the picture. In the center, surrounded by attendants and playmates, Princess Margarita poses. The king and queen appear in a mirror in the back. Studying light and its effects, Velázquez had painted Old World reality. Picasso painted the scene as a doll's house, creating an artificial reality. Painting most figures in Cubist style, some severely distorted, he did versions of the scene as a whole, of small groups, and of

Inspired by artist Diego Velázquez's Las Meninas
(*right*), *Picasso produced a series of forty-four paintings
in which he transformed the original. Picasso's* Las
Meninas (*above*) *distorted many of the figures in a
Cubist fashion, altering the reality of the work.*

individuals. He used dark shadows, Spanish reds and yellows, and subtle pastels. In
1968 he donated the entire series to the Picasso Museum in Barcelona.

In 1958, when Picasso wanted to get
away from the crowds of people trying to
see him in Cannes, he bought Château de
Vauvenargues near Aix-en-Provence,
about seventy-five miles west of Cannes
near Marseilles. The château was a
massive, noble house that fit into the bare
landscape and wooded hillsides. Picasso

moved the pictures from the bank vaults in Paris and sculptures from La Californie to this house. When it was remodeled and he had moved in, Picasso found that crowds of people stood on the hills peering at him through binoculars. Consequently, he and Jacqueline never settled in permanently at Vauvenargues but divided time between this house and La Californie.

Picasso at Eighty

On March 2, 1961, in a secret civil ceremony in Vallauris, Picasso married Jacqueline Roque, who was thirty-five at the time. Later that year he bought a new villa, Nôtre-Dame-de-Vie, which means Our Lady of Life. Because investors had begun building high-rises that blocked their view at La Californie, and because sightseers had invaded both of their houses, Picasso bought an isolated 250-year-old villa in Mougins, a town inland from Cannes and Vallauris. In October Picasso turned eighty and attended several birthday celebrations for him in Nice and Vallauris. The name of his new villa, de Vie, seemed especially appropriate.

By this time Picasso was very famous and very rich. After Jacqueline officially became his wife, she protected him from the hordes of people who wanted something from him. They distracted him and wasted his time and energy. Biographer Patrick O'Brian describes the intrusions:

Scores and even hundreds of people from all over the world wanted help, advice, introductions, encouragement; many of them were interesting or pathetic creatures, and Picasso's kindness was assailed on every side. There were also those who wanted him to collaborate on an article that would explain his painting, to write a preface, to illustrate a book, or to support a movement against poverty, war, and injustice, to say nothing of those whose eager search would be satisfied with a free picture, a comfortable sum of money, or even an autograph. Even after all these years of paying for his notoriety Picasso still often tried to see each member of the horde as an individual; but the numbers made it impossible. [69]

Picasso told his friend Brassaï that he would not wish his fame on anyone, not even an enemy.

Picasso was as rich as he was famous. Money came in from all sides as his paintings sold for higher and higher prices. He became the richest painter who had ever lived, but money no longer meant anything to him, once he had enough. Picasso lost track of exchange rates and seldom knew how much anything cost. O'Brian writes: "In restaurants Jacqueline always dealt with the bill, and when by some unusual chance he had to pay for anything himself he would take a large note from the wad he carried in his pocket, still fastened with a safety pin, after all these years, and sweep up the change." [70]

After the first picture of Jacqueline as Madame Z, painted in June 1954, Picasso continued to do many works with her as his model. In 1962 and 1963 alone he did over 160 Jacquelines. The original portrait was renamed *Portrait of Jacqueline with Clasped Hands*. Painted at the same time and in the same style is *Jacqueline aux Fleurs* (1954), in which she sits poised in a red

Portrait of Jacqueline with Clasped Hands *was Picasso's original painting of his wife. Inspired by her beauty, he painted over 160 portraits, depicting different poses and moods.*

chair near white flowers against a blue background. Both pictures show her large eyes, though each catches a different mood. He presented her in realistic style in *Portrait of Jacqueline with a Black Kerchief* (1955) and *Portrait of Jacqueline* (1955). Inspired by her beauty and her love, Picasso painted her face in many of his series paintings. At Nôtre-Dame-de-Vie, Picasso painted her in Cubist style in *Seated Woman with Yellow and Green Hat* (1962), a painting done in yellow, red, green, and blue. The figure has one green and one red eye facing front and a blue mouth and chin in profile. In *Portrait of Jacqueline* (1964), she sits in a chair holding a black kitten. While the head has a realistic style, the chair and her body are in Cubist style.

The early 1960s was a contented time for Picasso. He had expanded Nôtre-Dame and built a new studio. He painted there and worked on pots in Vallauris. He liked modern technologies and had a telephone installed in every bedroom. He bought a white Lincoln Continental and hired a chauffeur. His friends visited. He had a beautiful, devoted, and loving wife, who kept most unwanted intruders away. In the summer his house was full of children: Claude and Paloma, Jacqueline's daughter Kathy, Isabelle Leymarie, daughter of Jacqueline's friend, and Pablito and Marina, his son Paulo's children. The autumn weather in the south of France was unusually beautiful. Although he was eighty-three, it seemed that life was wonderful and would go on and on.

Picasso's Fortune Changes

But Picasso had seen his whole life alternate between high and low periods, and his fortune changed again. Late in 1964 rumors spread that Françoise Gilot was about to publish a book that would damage Picasso's reputation. It appeared early in 1965 in English, in which it was originally written, and in translations in French, Spanish, and German. Titling it *Life with Picasso*, Françoise wrote the book with Carlton Lake. Biographer Patrick O'Brian calls it "a nasty piece of work, nastier the more one reads it," and he quotes the newspaper *Le Monde*'s review: "a scandal-mongering production in which she recounts her private life, often quite without shame."[71] Many distinguished artists signed a public protest calling the book inaccurate, and many painters refused to exhibit their

Françoise Gilot displays her book Life with Picasso. *Considered an attempt to ruin Picasso's reputation, many artists protested the book, and Françoise.*

Neither his illness nor the scandal of Françoise's book, however, affected the plans already under way for Picasso's eighty-fifth birthday celebration. In 1966 the Musée National d'Art Moderne in Paris put on a great retrospective organized by Jean Leymarie, "Hommage à Picasso," an exhibit of Picasso's works from every period and every style. Three museums exhibited his work: in one his paintings, in another his drawings, sculpture, and ceramics, and in a third his prints. Between November 1966 and February 1967 nearly a million people saw the exhibitions. Since many works belonged to Picasso, they had never been seen before, particularly his sculptures. Picasso, however, continued to work quietly at Nôtre-Dame and did not

Picasso's rage over Françoise Gilot's book extended to his children. After the book was published, he ended his relationship with both Claude and Paloma, pictured here during an earlier, happier time.

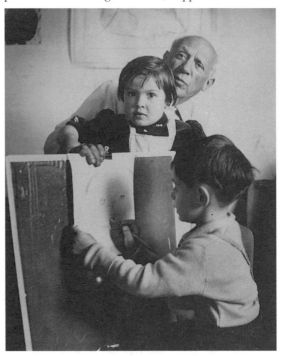

paintings if Françoise was to exhibit hers at the same location.

Angered at having his private life exposed again, Picasso was even more distressed than he had been when Fernande Olivier published her book in 1933. She had exposed Picasso's youth, but this book exposed Françoise's version of his adult life. His lawyers had tried to have the book's production stopped, but they lost the case, and the publicity increased sales. The publication strengthened Picasso's bitterness toward Françoise and extended to their children. He never saw Claude or Paloma again. To add to his misery, Picasso had to have ulcer surgery, an upsetting experience for a man who hated illness and death. Fortunately, the surgeons found no malignancy.

see the show. "Hommage à Picasso" continued into 1967 and traveled to London, New York, Dallas, and Fort Worth.

Praise for Picasso's work continued with new exhibitions and new publications discussing his art. In 1970 Barcelona opened the Picasso Museum in an area of the city where he had lived and worked. His friend Jaime Sabartés had suggested the idea for the museum in 1963 when he donated the works Picasso had given him. When Sabartés died in 1968, Picasso donated the entire series of *Las Meninas*, portraits of Jacqueline and Sabartés, pictures from La Californie, and a copy of every engraving from 1968 on. Early in 1970, Picasso's family donated boxes of his childhood drawings; today, the museum displays them.

Creative Energy of the Aging Artist

Amid all his other work, Picasso found time for another series on the artist and model. These works cover a period from 1959 to the end of his life. He used the theme to resolve contradictions in his life, to go beyond conflict by bringing harmony to art itself. In paintings and drawings and prints he presents the painter and his model, woman and her image, lover and his beloved, picador and the bull: image after image in which figures confront what is unfamiliar or face one another in unresolved opposition. Finally the model and the image merge as if what the painter sees has become one with what the painter creates.

In his eighty-eighth year Picasso painted 165 pictures, many of them 6 feet by 4, and introduced a new character—the musketeer. His musketeers are proud and fierce, armed with swords and guns, wearing mustaches and beards. In addition, he brought back circus people and matadors from the bullring. In these late-life paintings, he used bright colors in abundance—blues, greens, Spanish reds and yellows—and black to make strong lines.

Christian Zervos, who cataloged Picasso's works, and his wife Yvonne persuaded Picasso to show these works. Yvonne Zervos organized an exhibition in the Palace of the Popes, part of a festival in Avignon in southern France. Biographer Jean-Luc Duval reports the public's reaction and Picasso's comments about this exhibition:

> It came as a revelation. The public was astounded by the creative vitality of a man eighty-eight who had never seemed so young. . . .The figures in the Avignon paintings are often musketeers. "In these musketeers," [Picasso] says, "we may see ourselves. They sound the secret depths of men who, in their loneliness, their courage, their disappointments, find themselves bound by a common brotherhood which means much to them."[72]

In October 1971 Picasso turned ninety years old, another occasion for exhibitions. The Louvre rehung part of its collection to show eight Picasso paintings. This marked the first time that the work of a living artist was exhibited there. In New York an exhibition covered his work spanning seventy years. At the Tate Gallery in London schoolchildren gathered on the steps carrying a reproduction of Picasso's *Child Holding a Dove* (1901). They released ninety pigeons to mark Picasso's ninety years. During the celebrations Picasso continued to work at Nôtre-Dame-de-Vie.

In his last years Picasso lived a detached life at Nôtre-Dame. As most of his friends had died, he was content just working in his studio, making etchings and ink washes, mostly in black and white. During the winter of 1972–1973, he contracted influenza, from which he recovered, but he was left weak. Still he went on working and making plans for another show. On April 7, 1973, he had friends in for dinner, but he felt breathless when he went to bed. The local doctor came, detected a lung infection, and called Picasso's Paris doctor, who flew in the next morning. On April 8 Picasso rose, shaved, and was about to show the doctor some pictures in his studio, but he again became short of breath and had to lie down. Over the next hours he drifted painlessly in and out of sleep. At one time when he was awake, he told the doctor, who was single, "You are wrong not to marry. It's useful."[73] And he took Jacqueline's hand. Just before noon his heart failed, and he died. On April 10 Jacqueline had him buried at Vauvenargues in a simple ceremony with only a priest, his son Paulo, and a few friends present. Jacqueline had a 1933 statue, *Woman with Vase*, placed on his grave.

In celebration of his ninetieth birthday, many of Picasso's works were exhibited around the world. In London, schoolchildren gathered at the steps of the Tate Gallery carrying reproductions of Child Holding a Dove. *Subsequently, ninety pigeons were released in honor of Picasso's birthday.*

9 Picasso's Influence

Picasso died quietly and privately on April 8, 1973, at the age of ninety-one years, five months, and fourteen days. Though his end was uneventful, his life and his legacy have had a profound effect on art in the twentieth century. Art dealer Kahnweiler says, "The genius of Pablo Picasso has illuminated our century like a comet."[74]

Picasso not only revolutionized art, he was also extremely prolific. According to one estimate, he produced an average of one piece of art every day from the time he was eight years old.

Picasso's genius manifested itself in many ways, one of which was his large output of work. According to an estimate reported by one biographer, Picasso painted more than fifteen thousand canvases, in addition to his prints, sculptures, drawings, and ceramics. Given his long life and his prodigious output, a rough estimate suggests that Picasso averaged a piece of art every day from the time he was eight years old.

Picasso's genius also manifested itself in his ability to see and to use his hand to execute what he saw. Picasso was famous for the gaze of his dark, piercing eyes, as if he looked clear through what he focused on. His friend Paul Éluard called them "black diamonds" and said they never seemed to close. Art critic Michel Leiris, noting that Picasso's recurring theme of an artist and his model is about seeing, says, "*To have known how to see in that way:* this was the stroke of genius."[75]

According to Sabartés, Picasso could focus all his senses on an object as if he were in a spell. And then his imagination transformed what he saw, and his hand created it. Jean Sutherland Boggs, director of the National Gallery in Ottawa, Canada, says, "Picasso was an artist of such consummate skill, so at ease with his medium—any medium—that he could clown with it, pinching the neck of a vase in wet clay to make it a dove, while saying, 'You see, to make a dove you must first wring its neck.'"[76] For Picasso, art was an ongoing discovery, and in old age he was still striving to discover, as if he had much to find. He had mastered almost every medium but tapestry, an art form he had still hoped to learn.

Moreover, Picasso's genius manifested itself in a range of emotions that he expressed with great power. He had once called his childhood biscuit tin a symbol of feelings and moods. Biographer Pierre Daix says:

> Nothing is closer to life than Picasso's work, nothing closer to the truth. His portraits reveal suffering, happiness, love; but this revelation is never static; love is born, triumphs, is defeated; beauty blossoms in joy and is destroyed in anguish. . . . In his work things cry out, laugh, sleep, are at peace or at war, and are always alive— as alive as the eye that rests on them.[77]

Picasso's Vision

And finally, Picasso's genius manifested itself in his vision. In the preface to Brassaï's book *Picasso and Company*, Henry Miller speaks of Picasso's "extraordinary awareness" and says, "He not only sees and understands what is going on in this mad world, but he *foresees*. He not only gives the shape of things to come, but the feel as well. Without his presence in our midst one feels that the world would be rudderless."[78]

The vision Miller alludes to evolved because Picasso insisted on freedom to transform what he saw in the way he wanted. It evolved from his objectivity, from his presentation of horror and ugliness along with beauty and tranquility. It evolved from his interest in human beings and the way he learned how to look at them and how to look at himself. It evolved because he confronted the unresolved opposites in life. The whole body of Picasso's art makes a personal myth, with the painter as hero. Biographer Pierre Daix calls Picasso's work "a new measure of life. 'I don't develop,' Picasso once said, 'I am.' For him, being is to paint, to create, to transform—to transform himself, to create himself. In short, to live."[79]

Picasso was aware of his own genius, but he was not blinded by it. Henry Miller quotes Picasso:

> I have nothing but my genius to sustain me. Away with your illusions and delusions! I offer you grandeur, nobility, courage, daring. I ask for no better, no higher life. I am what I do, and vice versa. Take it or leave it. . . . I do what I must. Not what I ought to do, not even what I would like to do. I do, that is all.[80]

Nor did he lose his humility. Reflecting on himself, he told a friend, "I have never done anything extraordinary." To explain why he shut himself in his studio, he said, "What can I do? I have no choice but to *earn* my life."[81]

Picasso's Influence

Besides the power of his personal genius, Picasso redirected the history of twentieth-century art. The innovations of Cubism

Pictured in the studio in Vallauris, Picasso creates his last ceramic piece. Although best known for his paintings, Picasso mastered the art of ceramics, sculpture, print, and drawing.

changed a long-standing tradition in Western painting. For centuries painters had found many ways to depict external reality on the flat surface of a canvas. Without imitating, Picasso depicted a new kind of reality in a new way. According to Robert Rosenblum, Analytic Cubism destroyed the "traditional representations of light and shadow, mass and void, flatness and depth" and reconstructed them.[82] By a process of abstraction Picasso analyzed and simplified what he observed and broke up space into angular wedges or facets, a method he first presented in *Les Demoiselles d'Avignon*. When he introduced outside materials that both present them-

selves and represent something else, he went further in changing traditional art. This Synthetic Cubism, first seen in *Still Life with Chair Caning*, "is a true landmark in the history of painting," according to art critic Janson.[83] It is a landmark because real objects appear in paintings, while in traditional painting they were painted as if they were real. Picasso had effected these changes in painting by the time he was thirty years old.

He brought further changes to art by presenting two views of the same object in one picture. In reality a viewer would see two views at different times; in Picasso's pictures they are seen at the same time.

Art critic Alfred H. Barr Jr. sees a relationship to Albert Einstein's physics:

> This introduction of a time element into an art usually considered in terms of two- or three-dimensional space suggests some relationship to Einstein's theory of relativity in which time is thought of mathematically as a fourth dimension. Such comparisons between art and science are not precise; yet there are certain interesting analogies between Cubism and the space-time continuum of modern physics.[84]

Picasso's *Girl Before a Mirror* illustrates the technique of presenting two views at once. Picasso shows the figure's face in both frontal view and in profile and presents her and her reflected image in one picture.

Although Picasso's innovations first shocked both artists and viewers, thousands of artists and designers, and even architects, have been influenced by Cubism, and millions of viewers have attended his exhibitions. Cubism spread throughout the Western world. Some followers saw Cubism as a kind of precise geometry, a machinelike process that they applied to painting and sculpture. Other followers saw Cubism as a way to show the relationships of shapes in space, and they created circles and rectangles in colors. Others brought ordinary, real objects—soup cans and stuffed-fabric French fries—into their work, a style known as Pop Art. While others imitated Cubism or took it in new directions, Picasso went on to new ways of painting. Picasso's friend, Paul Éluard, sums up Picasso's influence on twentieth-century art in these words, reported by biographer Pierre Daix:

> Picasso knows that the man who goes forward discovers new horizons at every step! The result has been the opening up of new horizons, more than to any other painter before this twenty-five-year-old prodigy deliberately turned his back on everything he found ready to hand.[85]

To his time in history, Picasso gave his art, as Alfred H. Barr Jr. called it, "a visual symbol of the human spirit in its search for truth, freedom and perfection."[86]

Notes

Introduction: Revolutionizing Art

1. Quoted in Dore Ashton, *Picasso on Art: A Selection of Views.* New York: Viking Press, 1972.

2. Patrick O'Brian, *Picasso: Pablo Ruiz Picasso: A Biography.* New York: G. P. Putnam's Sons, 1976.

Chapter 1: Childhood, Youth, and Art Education, 1881–1898

3. Quoted in O'Brian, *Picasso.*

4. O'Brian, *Picasso.*

5. Arianna Stassinopoulos Huffington, "Creator and Destroyer," *The Atlantic Monthly,* June 1988.

6. Hélène Seckel, *Musée Picasso: Visitor's Guide.* Paris: Reunion des Musées Nationaux, 1993.

7. Quoted in O'Brian, *Picasso.*

8. Quoted in Pierre Daix, *Picasso.* New York: Frederick A. Praeger, 1965.

Chapter 2: The Maturing Artist, 1898–1905

9. Quoted in O'Brian, *Picasso.*

10. Daix, *Picasso.*

11. O'Brian, *Picasso.*

12. Quoted in Jean-Luc Duval, *Picasso: The Artist of the Century.* Biographical notes by Jean Leymarie. New York: Viking Press, 1971.

13. O'Brian, *Picasso.*

14. Alfred H. Barr Jr., *Picasso: Fifty Years of His Art.* New York: Museum of Modern Art, 1964.

15. Quoted in Barr, *Picasso.*

16. Quoted in O'Brian, *Picasso.*

Chapter 3: Cubism: A New Art Form, 1905–1912

17. Brassaï, *Picasso and Company.* Translated by Francis Price. Garden City, NY: Doubleday & Company, 1966.

18. Quoted in Brassaï, *Picasso and Company.*

19. Barr, *Picasso.*

20. Barr, *Picasso.*

21. Quoted in O'Brian, *Picasso.*

22. Daix, *Picasso.*

23. Quoted in Frank Elgar and Robert Maillard, *Picasso.* Translated by Francis Scarfe. New York: Frederick A. Praeger, 1956.

24. Quoted in O'Brian, *Picasso.*

25. Barr, *Picasso.*

26. William Rubin, *Picasso: In the Collection of the Museum of Modern Art.* New York: Museum of Modern Art, 1972.

27. O'Brian, *Picasso.*

28. Quoted in Ashton, *Picasso on Art.*

Chapter 4: Collages, Ballet, and a Turning Point, 1912–1922

29. Seckel, *Musée Picasso.*

30. Quoted in Duval, *Picasso.*

31. O'Brian, *Picasso.*

32. Quoted in O'Brian, *Picasso.*

33. Elgar and Maillard, *Picasso.*

34. Daix, *Picasso.*

35. Quoted in Ashton, *Picasso on Art.*

36. Quoted in Ashton, *Picasso on Art.*

37. Quoted in Ashton, *Picasso on Art.*

38. H. W. Janson with Dora Jane Janson, *History of Art: A Survey of the Major Visual Arts from the Dawn of History to the Present Day.* 2nd ed. Englewood Cliffs, NJ: Prentice-Hall, 1977.

39. Janson, *History of Art.*

40. O'Brian, *Picasso.*

41. Quoted in Daix, *Picasso.*

42. O'Brian, *Picasso.*

43. Seckel, *Musée Picasso.*

44. Quoted in Ashton, *Picasso on Art.*

Chapter 5: Post-Cubism Picasso, 1922–1936

45. Quoted in O'Brian, *Picasso.*

46. Janson, *History of Art.*

47. Quoted in O'Brian, *Picasso.*

48. O'Brian, *Picasso.*

Chapter 6: War and Guernica, 1936–1945

49. Quoted in Daix, *Picasso.*

50. Quoted in O'Brian, *Picasso.*

51. Quoted in O'Brian, *Picasso.*

52. Daix, *Picasso.*

53. Seckel, *Musée Picasso.*

54. Elgar and Maillard, *Picasso.*

55. Quoted in Alan Bowness, "Picasso's Sculpture," in Sir Roland Penrose and Dr. John Golding, eds., *Pablo Picasso: 1881–1973.* New York: Portland House, 1988.

56. Seckel, *Musée Picasso.*

57. Quoted in Seckel, *Musée Picasso.*

58. O'Brian, *Picasso.*

Chapter 7: Fame and Wealth, 1945–1954

59. O'Brian, *Picasso.*

60. Quoted in Dor de la Souchère. *Picasso in Antibes.* Translated by W. J. Strachan. New York: Pantheon, 1960.

61. Daix, *Picasso.*

62. Quoted in Jean Sutherland Boggs, "The Last Thirty Years," in Penrose and Golding, eds., *Picasso.*

63. Seckel, *Musée Picasso.*

64. Quoted in O'Brian, *Picasso.*

65. Daix, *Picasso.*

66. Quoted in Daix, *Picasso.*

Chapter 8: A Bountiful Old Age, 1954–1973

67. O'Brian, *Picasso.*

68. Quoted in Duval, *Picasso.*

69. O'Brian, *Picasso.*

70. O'Brian, *Picasso.*

71. Quoted in O'Brian, *Picasso.*

72. Duval, *Picasso.*

73. Quoted in O'Brian, *Picasso.*

Chapter 9: Picasso's Influence

74. Daniel-Henry Kahnweiler, "Introduction: A Free Man," in Penrose and Golding, eds., *Pablo Picasso.*

75. Michel Leiris, "The Artist and His Model," in Penrose and Golding, eds., *Pablo Picasso.*

76. Boggs, "The Last Thirty Years."

77. Daix, *Picasso.*

78. Quoted in Brassaï, *Picasso and Company.*

79. Daix, *Picasso.*

80. Quoted in Brassaï, *Picasso and Company.*

81. Quoted in Daix, *Picasso.*

82. Robert Rosenblum, "Picasso and the Typography of Cubism," in Penrose and Golding, eds., *Pablo Picasso.*

83. Janson, *History of Art.*

84. Alfred H. Barr Jr., *What Is Modern Painting?* New York: Museum of Modern Art, 1946.

85. Quoted in Daix, *Picasso.*

86. Barr, *What Is Modern Painting?*

For Further Reading

H. H. Arnason, *History of Modern Art: Painting, Sculpture, Architecture.* Englewood Cliffs, NJ: Prentice-Hall, and New York: Harry N. Abrams. A thorough analysis of modern art from the Impressionists through the mid-twentieth century with 1,393 illustrations and an extensive section on the Cubists and Picasso.

Alfred H. Barr Jr., *Cubism and Abstract Art.* Cambridge, MA: Harvard University Press, 1986. An explanation of the art that preceded Cubism, analysis of Analytic and Synthetic Cubism, and Cubism's influence on artists and art forms, with many black-and-white photographs, particularly of Picasso's works.

Lourdes Cirlot, *The Key to Modern Art of the Early Twentieth Century.* Minneapolis, MN: Lerner Publications, 1990. A short collection of artists and works typical of the twentieth century. Although only a few of Picasso's works have been included, the book puts Picasso in the context of his century.

Arthur C. Danto, "Picasso's Still Lifes," *The Nation,* October 5, 1991. An article commenting on recent attention given to Picasso: an exhibition of Picasso's still lifes, the publication of a new biography, and a review of the Musée Picasso in Paris.

Michael C. Fitzgerald, "Picasso: In the Beaux Quarters," *Art in America,* December, 1992. An article reviewing an exhibition of Picasso's still lifes, with discussion of particular paintings and the possible influence of Renoir on Picasso's still lifes.

Edward Lucie-Smith, *Lives of the Great Twentieth-Century Artists.* New York: Rizzoli International, 1986. The Picasso section provides key facts about Picasso's life and an explanation of major Cubist works, while placing Picasso in the context of his contemporaries and those he influenced.

Patricia A. MacDonald, *Pablo Picasso.* Englewood Cliffs, NJ: Silver Burdett Press, 1990. An easy-to-read book telling about Picasso's life and art, with black-and-white photographs and an insert of eight color prints.

Bernard S. Meyers and Trewin Copplestone, *The History of Art: Architecture, Painting, and Sculpture.* New York: Exeter Books, 1985. A thorough history of art from cave paintings through the twentieth century, with a section on Cubism and Picasso.

"Picasso," *Art and Man,* March 3, 1973. An article explaining Picasso's attitudes toward art and his approach to it, illustrated with a wide variety of works.

The Picasso Museum, Paris: Paintings, Papiers Collés, Picture Reliefs, Sculptures, and Ceramics. Translated by Alexander Lieven. New York: Henry N. Abrams, 1986. Many color photographs of the museum's extensive collection of Picasso works, with black-and-white photographs of many others. Also includes lists of Picasso's one-person exhibitions and a thorough chronology of Picasso's life.

Ernest Raboff, *Pablo Picasso*. New York: Harper & Row, 1982. A short, easy -to-read book explaining several of Picasso's paintings and drawings, mostly of children.

John Richardson, *A Life of Picasso*. 4 vols. New York: Random House, 1991. A thorough biography and explanation of Picasso's art, heavily illustrated with photographs of works.

Cesareo Rodriguez-Aguilera, *Picasso in Barcelona*. Barcelona: Ediciones Polígrafa, 1975. A collection of photographs compiled before Picasso gave his works to the museum, with an explanation of Picasso's life in Barcelona and the city's influence on him.

Robert Rosenblum, *Cubism and Twentieth-Century Art*. New York: Harry N. Abrams, 1982. A book presented in three parts: the foundation of Cubism, featuring Picasso and Braque; the expansion of Cubism in Paris; and the influence of Cubism on twentieth-century art.

Additional Works Consulted

Dore Ashton, *Picasso on Art: A Selection of Views*. New York: Viking Press, 1972. A collection of Picasso's comments on art, gathered from articles, books, and interviews, since Picasso himself wrote almost nothing about art.

Alfred H. Barr Jr., *Picasso: Fifty Years of His Art*. New York: Museum of Modern Art, 1964. A book providing biographical information and commentary on Picasso's art from his childhood drawings through his 1945 work, illustrated with many photographs. Appendixes include two of Picasso's statements about art and lists of theater works, exhibits, works in American museums, and a chronology of places where Picasso lived.

———, *What Is Modern Painting?* New York: Museum of Modern Art, 1946. A booklet that explains how to understand a painting, gives the history of modern painting, and explains Cubism and its effect on art.

Jean-Noël Beyler, *Orsay: The Museum and Its Collections*. Paris: Nuit et Jour, n.d. A book about the Musée d'Orsay's collection of Impressionist paintings, with photographs and descriptions of the artists.

Wilhelm Boeck and Jaime Sabartés, *Picasso*. New York: Harry N. Abrams, 1957. A collection of color photographs of the artist's works and a narrative about Picasso's personal life and his art written by Sabartés, who was Picasso's close friend.

Brassaï, *Picasso and Company*. Translated by Francis Price. Garden City, NY: Doubleday & Company, 1966. A collection of personal events and conversations involving Picasso, written by Picasso's friend.

Xavier Costa Clavell, *Picasso: Picasso Museum, Barcelona*. 7th ed. Barcelona: Editorial Escudo de Oro, 1992. A book of photographs from the museum's collection and a biographical commentary about Picasso's personal life and his art.

Pierre Daix, *Picasso*. New York: Frederick A. Praeger, 1965. A biography of Picasso's personal life and commentary about selected works, written by a man who was in close contact with Picasso between 1945 and 1965.

Jean-Luc Duval, *Picasso: The Artist of the Century*. Biographical notes by Jean Leymarie. New York: Viking Press, 1971. A book divided into two parts, the first part containing color photographs of Picasso's works with comments and opinions, and the second part containing biographical information.

Frank Elgar and Robert Maillard, *Picasso*. Translated by Francis Scarfe. New York: Frederick A. Praeger, 1956. A book containing Elgar's analysis of selected works and Maillard's biography of Picasso to age seventy.

Françoise Gilot and Carlton Lake, *Life with Picasso*. New York: McGraw-Hill, 1964. Gilot's personal impressions of Picasso and her view of their life together.

Edith Hamilton, *Mythology*. New York: New American Library, 1942. A classic that retells stories from Greek mythology.

Arianna Stassinopoulos Huffington, "Creator and Destroyer," *The Atlantic Monthly*, June 1988. An article portraying Picasso as a man whose thoughts and behavior had a dark side.

H. W. Janson with Dora Jane Janson, *History of Art: A Survey of the Major Visual Arts from the Dawn of History to the Present Day*. 2nd ed. Englewood Cliffs, NJ: Prentice-Hall, 1977. A large volume explaining trends and movements in art and contributions of individual artists, plus commentary about individual works; illustrated with photographs.

Michel Leiris, *Picasso and the Human Comedy: A Suite of 180 Drawings by Picasso*. New York: Random House, 1954. A collection of black-and-white photographs of Picasso's drawings and etchings of the artist and his model, with an introduction by Leiris.

James Lord, *Picasso and Dora: A Personal Memoir*. New York: Farrar, Strauss Giroux, 1993. An American's recollection of the time he met Picasso in Paris and the friendship he developed with Dora Maar.

Marilyn McCully, ed., *A Picasso Anthology: Documents, Criticism, Reminiscences*. Princeton, NJ: Princeton University Press, 1981. A collection of letters, exhibition reviews, personal accounts, and critical analysis covering Picasso's life and art from his early years to his death.

Patrick O'Brian, *Picasso: Pablo Ruiz Picasso: A Biography*. New York: G. P. Putnam's Sons, 1976. A biography covering Picasso's life from birth to death, providing the reader with background details, descriptions of Picasso's personal relationships, and comments about selected works.

Sir Roland Penrose and Dr. John Golding, eds., *Pablo Picasso: 1881–1973*. New York: Portland House, 1988. A collection of the following essays:

Jean Sutherland Boggs, "The Last Thirty Years."

Alan Bowness, "Picasso's Sculpture."

John Golding, "Picasso and Surrealism."

Daniel-Henry Kahnweiler, "Introduction: A Free Man."

Michel Leiris, "The Artist and His Model."

Roland Penrose, "Beauty and the Monster."

Theodore Reff, "Themes of Love and Death in Picasso's Early Work."

Robert Rosenblum, "Picasso and the Typography of Cubism."

Picasso: Dessins. Preface by Jean Bouret. Paris: Deux Mondes, 1950. A collection of black-and-white photographs of Picasso's drawings and etchings.

William Rubin, *Pablo Picasso: A Retrospective*. New York: Museum of Modern Art, 1980. An extensive photographic collection of Picasso's works from 1895 through 1970, with listings of chronological events interspersed throughout.

———, *Picasso: In the Collection of the Museum of Modern Art*. New York: Museum of Modern Art, 1972. Color photographs of the museum's Picasso collection, each accompanied by a critical analysis, plus photographs and notes about works found elsewhere.

Hélène Seckel, *Musée Picasso: Visitor's Guide*. Paris: Reunion des Musées Nationaux, 1993. Color photographs of a large number of the museum's works, each accompanied by a critical analysis, plus brief listings of events from Picasso's life.

Dor de la Souchère, *Picasso in Antibes*. Translated by W. J. Strachan. New York: Pantheon, 1960. Color photographs of the Picasso collection of the Antibes, France, museum and a narrative explaining how the museum came to be and how Picasso's art developed.

The Tate Gallery: An Illustrated Companion to the National Collections of British and Modern Foreign Art. London: The Tate Gallery, 1979. Color photographs of works from the museum's collection, each accompanied by a critical analysis, plus an explanation of each century's art history.

Index

Angel, The, 85
Apollinaire, Guillaume,
   39, 45, 48
aquatint, 63
Aragon, Louis, 81
art
   Cubism's influence on,
      95-97
   mediums of, 12-13, 36,
      39, 40, 45-46, 79, 95
   modernismo, 21, 23
   Picasso on, 12, 35, 44, 49,
      72, 79, 95
   realistic, 12, 16, 48
   reasons for, 12, 35, 40
artist
   definition of, 49
   Picasso on, 44
Ashton, Dore, 13, 44

Baboon and Young, 82
Balzac, Honoré de
   Picasso's illustrations for,
      55, 61
Barcelona, Spain
   effect on Picasso, 20-21
   Picasso Museum, 21, 88,
      92
Barr, Alfred H., Jr.
   comparing Cubism to
      relativity, 97
   description of Picasso,
      29
   on *Les Demoiselles
      d'Avignon*, 35, 38
Bateau-Lavoir, 28, 39
Bathers, 51
Bay at Cannes, The, 87
Blasco, José Ruiz (Picasso's

father)
   death of, 45
   influence on Picasso, 13,
      15, 16, 18
   teaching art, 13, 15, 16,
      17-18, 20
Blue Room, The , 26-27
Boeck, Wilhelm, 18, 54
Boggs, Jean Sutherland,
   79, 94
Boy Leading a Horse, 32
Braque, Georges, 39, 47
   Cubism by, 41, 45
   as Fauve artist, 34
   on *Les Demoiselles
      d'Avignon*, 38
Brassaï
   photographs Picasso's
      sculptures, 58
   Picasso and Company,
      95
   quotes Picasso, 33, 35,
      85, 89
Buffon, Georges-Louis, 63
Bull, 77
bullfighting, 15, 16, 17, 18
Bust of a Woman, 58

Café Agile, 28
Casagemas, Carlos, 23, 24,
   25
Célestine, 27
Cézanne, Paul
   influence on Picasso, 24,
      33, 35, 40-41
Château d'Antibes
Château de Boisegeloup,
   58, 59, 64
Child Holding a Dove, 93

Claude and Paloma, 80
Clouzot, Henri-Georges,
   84
Cocteau, Jean, 50
collages, 45, 51
Communist Party, 75, 81
Congress of Intellectuals
   for Peace, 75
Cranach the Elder, Lucas,
   77
Cubism
   ballet of, 50
   Braque and, 41, 45
   Curvilinear, 58–59
   end of, 47
   High Analytic, 42-44, 45,
      51, 96
   influence on art, 95-97
   Picasso explores, 40-44,
      45-47, 51, 59, 87
   Picasso invents, 35, 43
   reactions to, 11-12, 38,
      41, 43, 44, 47, 48
   Synthetic, 45-47, 51, 96
Cubist Painters, The, 45
Cubists, 45, 48

Daix, Pierre, 20
   on Cubists, 48
   on *Guernica*, 66-67
   on Picasso, 24, 74, 78, 95
Dalí, Salvador, 55
*David and Bathsheba, After
   Cranach the Elder*, 77
da Vinci, Leonardo, 32
Degas, Edgar, 24
de la Souchère, Dor, 78
de Lazerme, Jacques, 84
Derain, André, 47

de Zayas, Marius, 53
Death's Head, 72
Diaghilev, Sergey, 50
Dream, The, 59
Dufy, Raoul, 34
Duval, Jean-Luc, 92

Els Quatre Gats (The Four Cats) Café, 21, 22, 23
Éluard, Nusch, 63
Éluard, Paul, 63, 64, 83, 94, 97
Ernst, Max, 55
Escuela de Artes y Oficios de San Telmo, 15
etching, process of, 63

Factory at Horta de Ebro, 41
Family of Saltimbanques, The
Fauve artists, 34, 38
Franco, Francisco, 64

Gallerie Rosenberg, 62
Gauguin, Paul, 24, 33
Gilot, Françoise
    biography of Picasso, 81, 90-91
    break with Picasso, 82–83, 84
    children with Picasso, 79, 80
    in Picasso's art, 76, 77, 79
Girl Before a Mirror, 59, 97
Girl Jumping Rope, 82
Girl with a Basket of Flowers, 33
Girl with a Mandolin, 42
Girl with Bare Feet, 19
Gogh, Vincent van, 24
Gris, Juan, 45
Guernica, 71

exhibition of, 67-68
making of, 64-66
reactions to, 66-67, 74
Guitar, 55

Head of a Bull, 72
Head of a Woman, 58
Hillside at La Californie, The, 87
Histoire naturelle, 63
Horta de Ebro, Spain
    effect on Picasso, 21-22, 39
Huffington, Arianna, 19
Humbert, Marcelle (Eva), 39-40, 45, 47-48

Instituto da Guarda, 17

Jacob, Max, 39, 48
Jacqueline aux Fleurs, 89
Jaime Sabartés, 69
Janson, H. W.
    on artists, 49
    on Picasso's style, 56, 96
Joie de Vivre (Matisse), 34
Joie de Vivre (Picasso), 78
Junyer, Carlos, 23

Kahnweiler, Daniel-Henry, 40, 42, 47, 85, 94
Kaklova, Olga
    death of, 84
    marriage to Picasso, 50, 54-55, 57, 59
    Picasso paints, 50
    son with Picasso, 51
Korean War, 80

La Californie, 84, 85, 89, 92
La Coruña, Spain
    effect on Picasso, 17-19

Lake, Carlton, 81, 90
La Lonja, Barcelona
    School of Fine Arts, 20
Las Meninas, 87, 92
La Toilette, 32, 34
Le Chef-d'oeuvre Inconnu, 61
Leiris, Michel
    on Picasso's art, 82, 83, 94
Le Moulin de la Galette, 24-25
Le Mystère Picasso, 84-85
Les Demoiselles d'Avignon, 55, 96
    description of, 35, 38
    first Cubist painting, 11, 35
    Picasso on, 37
    reactions to, 11, 35, 38
Le Tremblay-sur-Mauldre, 64
Leymarie, Isabell, 90
Leymarie, Jean, 47, 91
Life with Picasso, 81, 90-91
lithography, 76–77
Louvre, 24, 34, 92

Maar, Dora
    photographs *Guernica*, 65
    Picasso paints, 64, 68-69
    Picasso's companion, 63, 64, 72, 75
Madman, The, 28
Ma Jolie (Woman with a Zither or Guitar), 43
Málaga, Spain, 15
Malraux, André, 75
Man in a Cap, 20
Manolo, 23, 43
Man with a Sheep, 73, 80
Manyac, Pere, 24
Maternity with Orange, 80

Matisse, Henri, 33, 39, 71
    death of, 83
    influence on Picasso,
        34-35, 78, 83
    reaction to *Les Demoiselles
        d'Avignon*, 38
Maya with a Doll, 69
Miller, Henry, 95
Minotauromachy, The, 61
Miró, Joan, 55
modernismo, 21, 23
Morosov, Ivan, 33
Mourlot, Fernand, 76
Musée de Sculpture
    Comparée, 35
Musée Grimaldi, 78
Musée National d'Art
    Moderne, 91
Musée Picasso, 78, 82
Museum of Modern Art,
    85

Nazis
    occupation of Paris, 69-
        71, 73-74
    reaction to Picasso's art,
        70-71, 74
Nesjar, Carl, 85
Nonell, Isidro, 23, 24
Notre-Dame-de-Vie, 89, 90,
    91, 93

O'Brian, Patrick, 16, 23
    Catalonian proverb, 20
    compares Matisse and
        Picasso, 34–35
    description of childhood
        painting, 17
    on Fernande Olivier, 29
    on Françoise's
        biography, 90
    on Picasso film, 85
    on Picasso's children, 51

on Picasso's
    contribution to art, 14
on Picasso's fame, 89
on Picasso's strength, 26
Old Guitarist, The, 27
Olivier, Fernande, 34
    biography of Picasso, 59,
        91
    break with Picasso, 39
    describes Picasso, 29, 32
    description of, 29
    inspires Pink Period, 29
    meets Picasso, 29, 30
    Picasso uses as model,
        34, 39, 42

Painter with Model Knitting,
    61
painting
    collages, 45, 51
    Cubist, 12, 35
    Fauve, 34, 38
    Impressionist, 20, 21
    realistic, 12
    Surrealism, 55, 60
Pallarès, Manuel, 20, 21-22
Paris, France
    influence on Picasso, 24-
        31
    Nazi occupation of, 69-
        74
Paulo as Harlequin, 53
Peace, 80-81
Penrose, Roland, 88
Picasso, Claude (son) 79,
    90, 91
Picasso, Concepción
    (sister), 16, 18-19
Picasso, Lolita (Lola,
    sister), 16, 17
Picasso, Maria de la
    Concepción (Maya,
    daughter), 59, 69, 72,

73-74
Picasso, Marina
    (granddaughter), 90
Picasso, Pablito
    (grandson), 90
Picasso, Pablo
    African influences, 35-39
        on revelation of, 37
    animals and, 28
        as subjects, 17, 18, 20,
            22, 51, 63, 66, 73, 79,
            82
        pets of, 28, 30, 39, 63,
            72, 84
    on art, 12, 35, 44, 49, 72,
        79, 95
    art schools, 17-18, 20-21
        father teaches, 13, 16,
            17-18
    on beauty, 24
    biographies of
        by Brassaï, 95
        by Fernande Olivier,
            59, 91
        by Françoise Gilot, 81,
            90-91
    birth of, 15
    blending of styles, 51-52
    Blue Period, 26-28, 29,
        30, 62
    Bone Period, 60, 62
    book illustrations, 55,
        61, 63, 64
    character of, 13-14, 16
    childhood art, 16, 17
    children of, 51, 60, 69,
        79, 80
    classical themes, 13, 31-
        32, 33, 34, 51, 56, 58,
        61, 78, 80
    clay works, 79-80, 90
    as a collector, 17, 39, 54
    color use, 21, 38, 41, 42,

51, 53, 54, 59, 68-69, 79, 87, 88, 90, 92
comic book, 64
as Communist Party member, 75
Cubism and, 11-12, 35–36, 38, 40-44, 45-47, 50, 51, 58, 87, 95-97
quote on, 42, 47
death of, 93, 94
description of, 29
designs theater sets, 50-51
Dora Maar and , 63-65, 68-69, 72, 75
early life of, 13, 15-22
evolving techniques, 54-57
exhibitions, 19, 21, 62, 67, 75, 85, 91-93
"Hommage à Picasso," 91-92
fame of, 44, 54, 74, 75, 85, 89
family of, 15-16
father's influence on, 13, 15, 16, 18
Fernande Olivier and, 29-30, 32, 34, 39, 42, 59, 91
film about, 84-85
Françoise Gilot and, 76-78, 79, 80, 83-84, 90-91
on his genius, 95
illness of, 88, 93
Impressionist works, 20-21
influence on art, 11, 14, 94-97
intellectual groups, 21, 23, 28, 63
on La Lonja exams, 20
light, use of, 21, 22, 43,

51, 78, 87
lithographs, 76, 80
Marcelle (Eva) Humbert and, 39-40, 45, 47-48
Marie-Therese Walter and, 57-60, 62, 64, 68, 72, 73-74
marriages
to Jacqueline Roque, 84, 89-90
to Olga Kaklova, 50, 51, 54-55, 57, 59, 84
mediums of art, 12-13, 35, 39, 40, 45-46, 79, 95
Negro Period, 39, 62
as an outsider, 17, 20, 32, 47
on painting, 13, 14
Paris and, 24-31, 69-74
patron of, 24
Pink Period, 29-31, 33, 62
posters, 21, 80, 81
poverty of, 25-28, 32
printmaking, 61
realist works, 12, 16, 48
sales of art, 24, 28, 33, 54
schooling of, 16
sculpture of, 39, 57-59, 82, 85, 89
signature of, 23
solitude of, 25-26, 30, 34, 87, 89
Spanish Civil War and, 64-67
on style, 52, 53
on success, 33-34
Surrealism and, 55, 60
volume of work, 12, 40, 76, 94
on *War* and *Peace*, 77
wealth of, 50, 54, 75, 89

works with Braque, 41, 45
during World War I, 47
during World War II, 69-74
Picasso, Paloma (daughter), 80, 90, 91
Picasso, Paulo (son), 51, 59, 90, 93
Picasso Museum, 88, 92
Picasso y Lopez, Maria (mother), 15, 67
Pigeons, The, 87
Pignon, Eduoard, 83
Pignon, Hélène Parmelin, 83
Poincaré, Henri, 43
Pop Art, 97
Portrait of Dora Maar, 68-69
Portrait of Jacqueline, 90
Portrait of Jacqueline with a Black Kerchief, 90
Portrait of Jacqueline with Clasped Hands, 89, 90
Portrait of Marie-Therese, 68-69
Portrait of Mm. Z, 83
Portrait of Nusch Éluard, 69
pottery, 79-80
printmaking, 61
Pushkin Museum, 33

Ramié, Georges, 79
Ramié, Suzanne, 79
Red Tablecloth, The, 54
Renoir, Pierre-Auguste
influence on Picasso, 24
Rilke, Rainer Maria, 30
Roque, Jacqueline, 84, 89-90
marriage to Picasso, 89
meets Picasso, 84
Picasso's death and, 93

Roque, Kathy, 84, 90
Rosenblum, Robert, 96
Rubin, William
    on *Ma Jolie*, 43
    on *Seated Bather*, 60
Ruiz, Diego (grandfather), 15
Rusiñol, Santiago, 23

Sabartés, Jaime
    at Els Quatre Gats, 23
    painting of, 69, 70, 92
    on Picasso's marriage to Olga, 50
    on Picasso's philosophy, 26
    on Picasso's talent, 18, 54, 94
    as secretary to Picasso, 59, 63
    suggests Picasso Museum, 92
Salmon, André, 38, 44
Sartre, Jean-Paul, 75
Satie, Erik, 50
Science and Charity, 20-21
sculpture, 39, 57-59, 72-73, 82, 85, 89
Seated Bather, 60-61
Seated Woman, 51
Seated Woman with Yellow and Green Hat, 90
Seckel, Hélène
    curator of Musée Picasso, 46
    describes Picasso's paintings, 19, 52, 69, 72-73, 82

explains Cubist point of view, 46, 51-52
Second World Conference of the Partisans of Peace, 81
Shchukine, Sergei, 33
She Goat, The, 82
Soulié, Père, 28
Spanish Civil War, 64-67
Stein, Gertrude, 33, 34, 39, 47
Stein, Leo, 33, 38, 39, 47
Still Life with Chair Caning, 45-46, 96
Student with a Pipe, 47
Sueño y Mentira de Franco, 64
Surrealism, 55, 60
Swimmer, The, 57

Tate Gallery, 85, 92
Three Bathers, 54
Three Dancers, 56
Three Dutch Women, 31
Three Musicians, 51
Toulouse-Lautrec, Henri-Marie-Raymond
    influence on Picasso, 24, 26
Two Acrobats with a Dog, 30

Uhde, Wilhelm, 42
Utrillo, Miguel, 23, 28

Vallauris, France, 79, 80, 84, 89, 90
van Gogh, Vincent, 24
Vauxcelles, Louis, 41

Velázquez, Diego, 87
Vollard, Ambroise
    buys Picasso pictures, 33
    death of, 67
    illustrations for Buffon's book, 63
    on *Les Demoiselles d'Avignon*, 38
    portrait by Picasso, 42, 48

Walter, Marie-Thérèse
    companion to Picasso, 57, 64, 72, 73-74
    daughter with Picasso, 59
    Picasso's portraits of, 57, 59, 62, 68-69
    sculptures by Picasso, 58
War, 77, 80
Wire Construction, 57
Woman Flower, 77
Woman in a Garden, 58
Woman in White, 53
Woman Ironing, The, 27
Woman with an Orange, 58
Woman with a Vase, 93
Woman with Leaves, 58
Woman with Outstretched Arms, 85
Woman with Pears, 42
World War I, 47
World War II, 69-74

Zervos, Christian, 63, 92
Zervos, Yvonne, 63, 92

Picture Credits

cover photo: FPG International

Alinari/Art Resource, NY, 88 (bottom)

© Archive Photos, 13, 29 (both), 50, 83, 84, 91 (both), 94

Art Resource, NY, 61, 65, 67

The Bettmann Archive, 63

Bridgeman/Art Resource, NY, 17

Family of Saltimbanques, Chester Dale Collection, © 1994 Board of Trustees, National Gallery of Art, Washington, 1905, canvas, 2.128 x 2.296 (83 ¾ x 90 ⅜); framed: 2.404 x 2.563 (94 ⅝ x 100 ⅞), 31

Giraudon/Art Resource, NY, 12, 19, 20, 24, 39, 40, 47, 49 (left), 53, 57, 59, 66, 68 (right), 69, 70, 73, 78, 80, 81, 87, 88 (top)

The Metropolitan Museum of Art, Bequest of Gertrude Stein, 1946. (47.106), 34

The Metropolitan Museum of Art, The Elisha Whittelsey Collection, The Elisha Whittlesey Fund, 1947. (47.140), 49 (right)

Pablo Picasso, *The Bathers*, Musée Picasso, © PHOTO R.M.N. SPADEM, 52

Pablo Picasso, *Bull's Head*. Musée Picasso, © PHOTO R.M.N. SPADEM, 72

Pablo Picasso, *Les Demoiselles d'Avignon*, 1907, oil on canvas, 8' x 7'8". The Museum of Modern Art, New York. Acquired through the Lillie P. Bliss Bequest. Photograph © 1994 The Museum of Modern Art, New York, 36

Pablo Picasso, *Françoise*, lithograph, 1946, 65 x 50 cm, Gift of Mr. Joseph R. Shapiro, 1955.560. Photograph © 1994, The Art Institute of Chicago, All Rights Reserved, 76

Pablo Picasso, *Girl Jumping Rope*, Musée Picasso, © PHOTO R.M.N. SPADEM, 82

Pablo Picasso, *Guitar*, 1926, Musée Picasso, © PHOTO R.M.N. SPADEM, 56 (top)

Pablo Picasso, *Jacqueline with Clasped Hands*, Musée Picasso, © PHOTO R.M.N. SPADEM, 90

Pablo Picasso, *Ma Jolie*, 1911-1912, oil on canvas, 39 ⅜" x 25 ¾". The Museum of Modern Art, New York. Acquired through the Lillie P. Bliss Bequest. Photograph © 1994 The Museum of Modern Art, New York, 42

Pablo Picasso, Maquette for Chicago Richard A. Daley Center Monument, welded steel sculpture, 1965, 105.4 x 69.9 cm, Gift of Pablo Picasso, 1966.379. Photograph © 1994, The Art Institute of Chicago, All Rights Reserved, 86

Pablo Picasso, *The Minotauromachy*, Musée Picasso, © PHOTO R.M.N. SPADEM, 62

Pablo Picasso, *The Old Guitarist*, oil on panel, 1903, 122.9 x 82.6 cm, Helen Birch Bartlett Memorial Collection, 1926.253. Photograph © 1994, The Art Institute of Chicago, All Rights Reserved, 28

Pablo Picasso, *Seated Bather*, 1930, oil on canvas, 64 ¼ x 51". The Museum of Modern Art, New York. Mrs. Simon Guggenheim Fund. Photograph © 1994 The Museum of Modern Art, New York, 60

Pablo Picasso, *Seated Woman*, Musée Picasso, © PHOTO R.M.N. SPADEM, 51

Pablo Picasso, *Third Vallauris Poster*, 1948, lithograph, printed in color, 22 ½" x 15 ⁷⁄₁₆". The Museum of Modern Art, New York. Gift of David-Henry Kahnweiler. Photograph © 1994 The Museum of Modern Art, New York, 79

Pablo Picasso, *Wire Construction*, Musée Picasso, © PHOTO R.M.N. SPADEM, 58

The Phillips Collection, Washington, D.C., 27

© Photo Arxiu Fotografic de Museus, Ajuntament de Barcelona, 21

© PHOTO R.M.N. SPADEM, Musée Picasso, 15, 16, 37

Reproduced by courtesy of the Trustees, The National Gallery, London, 93

© Roberto Otero/Black Star, 96

Scala/Art Resource, NY, 23, 25, 32, 46, 68 (left)

The Tate Gallery/Art Resource, NY, 56 (bottom)

UPI/Bettmann, 11, 71

About the Author

After many years of teaching composition and British literature, Clarice Swisher now devotes her time to research and writing. She is the author of *The Beginning of Language, Relativity,* and *The Importance of Albert Einstein.* She lives in Saint Paul, Minnesota.